The Gospels unplugged

Text copyright © Lucy Moore 2002
Illustrations copyright © Francis Blake 2002

The author asserts the moral right
to be identified as the author of this work

Published by
The Bible Reading Fellowship
First Floor, Elsfield Hall
15–17 Elsfield Way, Oxford OX2 8FG
ISBN 1 84101 243 2

First published 2002
10 9 8 7 6 5 4 3 2 1 0

Acknowledgments
Unless otherwise stated, scripture quotations are taken from the Contemporary English Version
© American Bible Society 1991, 1992, 1995. Used by permission/Anglicizations © British and
Foreign Bible Society 1997.

A catalogue record for this book is available from the British Library

Printed and bound in Malta

The Gospels unplugged

Lucy Moore

52 poems and stories for creative writing, RE, drama and collective worship

For Kirsten Hall, Elizabeth Hall, Sally Hall, Michael Hall, Sam Harvey and Phoebe Ainesaz, with much love

Thanks to…

Eric Guthrie for the love of rhyme; Sue Doggett for the wisdom culinary, piscicultural and editorial; Paul for being a theological sounding-board; Sue Smith for a teacher's eye; Crossroads Drama Group, especially Lesley Baker and Denise Williams, and the congregations at St Wilf's and Westbrook for being such willing and supportive testbeds; Karen and Lisa for the inspirational hygiene; the cast of The Mystery Tour *for happy memories. And, of course, to Matthew, Mark, Luke and John for doing the hard work.*

Contents

Foreword

When it comes to telling Bible stories, just about the worst thing we can do is to make them boring. The second worst thing, however, is to try so hard to make them 'fun' that we trivialize them. That place in the middle, where the story is told creatively in a fresh and vital manner, and yet still communicates God's love and truth, is the place that Lucy Moore has found in this book.

These re-tellings are hugely entertaining—bursting with inventiveness and wit. And this is a great help, particularly for those teachers and church workers who have told some of the more familiar stories time and time again. There's nothing better than discovering a new way 'in' to a story, or a different angle from which to tell it. This not only helps you to see the story in a fresh light, but it also creates a new enthusiasm for that tale—an enthusiasm that the children will hopefully catch as well. And so, Lucy not only offers us different points of view, but different literary forms, as well—mixing poetry and drama and rap—so that the audience never quite knows what to expect.

The fact that Lucy obviously enjoys telling these stories, and that children have a great time when they experience them, never obscures the equally important fact that there are some very serious things going on here. She deals with the hard issues of loving your neighbour, forgiveness, fear and temptation (just to name a few) with the honesty and gravity they deserve. And her introductions do an excellent job of tying the biblical text to her particular take on the story and then to questions that will help children to explore the story even further, in their own terms and from their own experience.

As far as I can tell, there are three things that are evident in this book. Lucy loves stories. Lucy loves kids. And Lucy loves God. It's just the right combination for a book like this. It's good—in every sense of that word. It's fun. And I think you're going to have 'good fun' using it!

Bob Hartman

Introduction

Have fun with *The Gospels unplugged*! The pieces have been great fun to write and perform and I hope you'll enjoy them too. The idea is that they will help bring the Gospels to life—make the stories jump off the page, into the imagination and from there into daily life. Each piece comes with a short introduction, partly so that you can see where I'm coming from, and partly to suggest some ideas for discussion raised by the passage, in case you want to take it further. You also have the relevant Bible passage for reference.

Of course it's been a nail-chomping job, deciding which passages to include. I've deliberately chosen many pieces that include children, bearing in mind the intended users of this book, but beyond that the passages try to reflect a balance between those that show us who Jesus is, what he did and what he said—history, actions, miracles and teaching, if you like. Some of the pieces, such as 'Zacchaeus', tell the story, while some, such as 'Jesus angry in the temple', explore an aspect of the original account.

While I've been writing, I've had in mind a fictional Key Stage 2 teacher who despairs of teaching RE, is fed up with the same old stories and wants something with a bit of bite, preferably that could be used in a drama or literacy session as well. I've had in mind a Year 6 class who've heard the Good Samaritan fifteen times now and are sure they've got Christianity taped. I've also had in mind church children's workers and youth leaders who know that their groups love drama and want a resource book that can be picked up and used at the drop of a hat. From school assemblies to all-age worship, I hope you will find something that will engage your audience and actors with the living power of the Gospel stories.

Some ideas for using the book: if you're reading to an audience, I'd suggest you read the *Gospels unplugged* version of the story, then read the words from the Bible, rather than the other way round. Photocopy the passage, and read it in parts like a script. Add some percussion if it's a rhythmic number, music or sound effects if it's atmospheric. Give your readers or listeners permission to *enjoy* what they're reading. Have a good laugh if it's that sort of piece; compare it with other styles of writing or other pieces written in the same style;

follow it up with people writing their own creative piece on the same subject, or drawing or painting to show the pictures it has inspired in their imaginations.

Many of the questions in the introductions are open-ended. I believe it's important for people to wonder, to want to find out answers for themselves and to realize that Christianity opens up huge areas of questioning. It's OK for the teacher or leader to say, 'I don't know'! (At least, I hope it is—I say it all the time.)

Teachers and church leaders have endless demands on their time and energy. That's why the Gospel passages are extensively indexed by reference and theme. (From experience, I know the need for *'something—anything!—on forgiveness, now!'* and the frustration of not being able to remember which pieces deal with which subjects.)

Many of the pieces, such as 'The paralysed man through the roof', work best in performance and look bizarrely colloquial on the page. Other pieces, such as 'Perfume', are too dense to be performed and work better enjoyed quietly. Some beg not to be taken too seriously—how much wisdom can you fit into a limerick, after all? Others, like 'The quiet man' (pp. 129–130), touch on the power, mystery and majesty that echo through the original Gospels. It's been a humbling experience, plunging into the work of these four great writers, and predictably they're an impossible act to follow. At best, this book is merely a snack, whetting the appetite for the real meal within their pages.

Many of the pieces in this book come from my work in schools and churches in association with the *Barnabas Live* programme, in which the creative arts—drama, movement and storytelling—are used in performance and workshops within primary schools to bring the Bible to life.

BRF also offers a roadshow, called *The Bible unplugged!* Suitable for libraries, churches, bookshops, festivals and so on, it combines a Bible-based drama workshop with a performance of Bible stories, like the ones in this book, for all ages. To find out more about either of these, write to Barnabas Ministry, BRF, First Floor, Elsfield Hall, 15 –17 Elsfield Way, Oxford OX2 8FG.

Why Luke wrote

LUKE 1:1–4

Many people have tried to tell the story of what God has done among us. They wrote what we had been told by the ones who were there in the beginning and saw what happened. So I made a careful study of everything and then decided to write and tell you exactly what took place. Honourable Theophilus, I have done this to let you know the truth about what you have heard.

Why did the Gospel writers write their books?

Luke probably wrote his book round about AD60 —only thirty years or so after Jesus died. Think of someone who died about thirty years ago. If you were writing a book about that person, how easy would it be to make people believe anything you wanted to tell them about him or her? What would you do to find out about your person? Why might you want to write a book about somebody you'd never met face to face?

Read this poem, then read the opening of Luke's book from the Bible: what was Luke trying to do? Do you trust him to tell 'the truth about what you have heard'?

Many people have tried to write
The story of what God has done among us. So I
Have watched and wondered and studied and read
And listened to what those who knew him said.
I have been a detective, a historian, never satisfied
With those who exaggerated, told part-truths, or lied.
A scientist, a doctor, a writer, I have done my best
To put each witness of those days to the test:
Questioned and queried and challenged and argued
With Mark, with all who knew him
Face to face, so that you'd
Know
The truth,
As far as

I can
Write
Truth,
About
This
Man
Called
Jesus.

THE GOSPEL ACCORDING TO LUKE

Reproduced with permission from *The Gospels unplugged* published by BRF 2002 (1 84101 243 2)

Annunciation

LUKE 1:26–38

God sent the angel Gabriel to the town of Nazareth in Galilee with a message for a virgin named Mary. She was engaged to Joseph from the family of King David. The angel greeted Mary and said, 'You are truly blessed! The Lord is with you.'

Mary was confused by the angel's words and wondered what they meant. Then the angel told Mary, 'Don't be afraid! God is pleased with you, and you will have a son. His name will be Jesus. He will be great and will be called the Son of God Most High…'

Mary asked the angel, 'How can this happen? I am not married!'

The angel answered, 'The Holy Spirit will come down to you, and God's power will come over you…'

Mary said, 'I am the Lord's servant! Let it happen as you have said.' And the angel left her.

We don't know much about Mary's background. She was probably a young teenager, and had a good relationship with God. So here she is, a modern teenager (when she says 'thank God' she means it!), just home from school, when she has an unexpected visit.

How do you imagine angels to be? Have you ever seen one? (Lots of people claim they have met angels.)

If you felt that God was calling you to a difficult, apparently impossible job that meant you'd be in danger, whispered about, gossiped about, cut off from your friends or worse, would you react like Mary? In the Bible she says, 'I am the Lord's servant! Let it happen as you have said.' Can you think of a time when it hasn't been easy to do what you believe is right?

Called goodbye to Kylie and Cherie.
Unlocked the door—no one home but me.
Made myself a milkshake, turned the CD up loud.
No French homework, phew, thank God.
And the Physics test was cancelled, even less to do.
Loosened my tie and kicked off my shoes.
Turned to get my magazine but stopped. Phased.
This angel was staring me right in the face.

I'm not talking a fairy off a Christmas tree.
This angel stooped to fit the room—was eight foot two or three,
Muscles like a fireman. If he'd spread his wings out more
They'd have smashed out both the window and the door.
Towering over me, shoulders arched high,
One flick of his finger and I'd be splatted like a fly.
The CD stopped. Felt like the silent room would burst.
Should you scream or pray at times like this? But Gabriel moved first.
Dropped down to his knees and bowed his head before me
And spoke—his voice like Andrex—some words to reassure me:

'Mary, feel God showering down on you like a rainbow.
The Lord is with you, by you, around you, in you.
Bask in him, dance with him, spin in him,
Relax into the peace he's bringing.'

Reproduced with permission from *The Gospels unplugged* published by BRF 2002 (1 84101 243 2)

What the heck was going on? An angel kneeling?
How can I describe the ice-cold panic I was feeling?
Was I about to die? 'No!' Gabriel went on.
'God is thrilled to bits with you. Wants you to have his Son.
You will call him Jesus. Highest heaven's king.
His kingdom will go on and on, never ending.'

'Me? Have God's baby? How can this be?
No man has ever even laid a finger on me!
I'm not married, though I'm going steady—
Hang on a minute—I don't think I'm ready…'

Gabriel rose up from the floor and spread his wings around me.
I thought that I'd drown in their perfume. Heaven surrounded me.
The white wings blinded, dazzled, and like widescreen there I saw
If I said 'yes', visions of glory, pain, the agony in store.

'God's Spirit will come down to you
And his power will come to rest in you.'
And I nodded, safe in that feather-light cuddle,
Certain that God would sort out the muddle
I knew was to come. 'I am in God's hands.
Whatever you say. Whatever he wants.'

And I was alone in the room once more
With a song on the hi-fi that I'd never heard before.

Reproduced with permission from *The Gospels unplugged* published by BRF 2002 (1 84101 243 2)

Christmas

MATTHEW 1:18—2:23; LUKE 2:1–21; JOHN 1:14

John writes:

The Word became a human being and lived here with us. We saw his true glory, the glory of the only Son of the Father. From him all the kindness and all the truth of God have come down to us.

I sometimes look at the news and secretly think, 'If I was God, I'd put an end to that terrible situation. Why doesn't he do anything?' But then I remember that God has plans for us all that reach further than anything I could imagine: 'My thoughts and my ways are not like yours. Just as the heavens are higher than the earth, my thoughts and my ways are higher than yours,' he explains in Isaiah 55:8.

What do you think Christmas is all about? I wonder, why didn't God just stay safe in heaven? Jesus came as a baby to a poor family—what does this tell you about God's view of ordinary people? What things on earth do you most want to change for the better?

The world would be a better place
If I was God!
I'd save the world!
(Save it from what?)
Oh you know, all the things that go wrong:
War, disease, ecological disaster, rice pudding.
(And how would you do it?)
I'd come down from heaven…
(Why?)
So that people could see me in action and know it was me!
(Fair enough. So how would you get here?)
I quite fancy a sparkly staircase
Like on a really classy quiz show.
No! A private jet and stretch limo
And bands playing, crowds cheering,
People desperate for my autograph,
Girls screaming, boys panting to get a glimpse of me,
Like a pop star, only better.
You know, old ladies would like me too.
(OK. And where would you go?)
The world's my lobster!
(Oyster.)
Be quiet. I'm God, remember?
So I'd probably go to the White House.
Or the Houses of Parliament.
Or a throne in Moscow, Delhi, Tokyo—
No! *All* of those and more. A huge palace in every city.
Where world leaders can come and grovel before me,
And I'd tell them how to rule their countries properly.
And that if they kept being greedy and selfish,
I'd blast them with thunderbolts
And give them horrible diseases.
(Hang on—you've come to save the world from those.)
But I need to show them I'm boss!
I'd turn their tanks into tractors.
(How?)
I'm God! I'm magic! I can break any rules I want!
I'd give all the money from the rich countries to the poor countries.
(But then you'd have to give it all back again.)
Look! I'm warning you!
I'd throw all the bad people into jail.
(How bad?)

Shut up! You for a start! I'm *God*! I decide!

And I'd mend the hole in the ozone layer and replant the rainforests and stop the flooding in Bangladesh and make graffiti disappear AND litter and clean up the oil slicks in the sea and neutralize all the nuclear waste and invent cars that run on water and not let people use bleach in their toilets AND I'd tell them the cure for AIDS and cancer and MS and colds and let them have chips every day and football every afternoon and I'd show everyone how to do space exploration and I'd cancel all the world debts and find all the orphans families AND make dodos come back to life and everyone would see I'm God and they'd really want to worship me. And there'd be pop and crisps after church services too. *(Yeah.*

Or you could send a baby
to a penniless family
of an ethnic minority
in a dead-end town
at the back of beyond
to be born in a backstreet slum
under foreign occupation,
make him a political refugee,
let him grow up a labourer
in the middle of nowhere
without a decent education
and expect him to save the world.)

Don't be daft.

Reproduced with permission from *The Gospels unplugged* published by BRF 2002 (1 84101 243 2)

Visit to the temple

Saturday story

LUKE 2:41–52

Every year Jesus' parents went to Jerusalem for Passover. And when Jesus was twelve years old, they all went there as usual for the celebration. After Passover his parents left, but they did not know that Jesus had stayed on in the city. They thought he was travelling with some other people, and they went a whole day before they started looking for him. When they could not find him with their relatives and friends, they went back to Jerusalem and started looking for him there.

Three days later they found Jesus sitting in the temple, listening to the teachers and asking them questions. Everyone who heard him was surprised at how much he knew and at the answers he gave.

When his parents found him, they were amazed. His mother said, 'Son, why have you done this to us? Your father and I have been very worried, and we have been searching for you!'

Jesus answered, 'Why did you have to look for me? Didn't you know that I would be in my Father's house?' But they did not understand what he meant.

One thing many Christians learn about God is that he's full of surprises! Remember what they say about Aslan in the *Narnia* books? 'It's not as if he's a tame lion.' Jesus was always doing the unexpected.

In this story the imaginary narrator, Jacob, says he was angry with Jesus because Jesus was always breaking rules. What do you think is the real reason Jacob was angry with him? When have you felt jealous of someone and why?

Why do we have rules? Is it ever right to break rules? What's the difference between the way Jacob sees religion and the way Jesus sees it?

We follow God's rules, Misha! Keep the rules and you'll keep out of trouble. It is as simple as that.

And you can see from yesterday what happens when you break the rules. Oh yes, he was a great rule-breaker, that Jesus. Always was. Did I tell you about the time we all came up to Jerusalem? Years ago, the year before I took my *bar mitzvah*—I must have been twelve. So he was too.

He was always a troublemaker. Even as a boy. Oh, he got away with it because he fooled people into liking him. Everybody liked Jesus. Can't think why. The whole village thought the sun shone out of his… yes. He was good-looking, I suppose. But he was always sucking up to people—spending hours talking to smelly old grannies who were frankly best forgotten; carving stupid toys out of wood for the village brats; helping

his mother round the house—women's work! And the hours he spent with my father—pretending to know so much about the Holy Books! Asking all these pretentious questions—oh, he was a real know-it-all, Jesus was. A dreamer too. I suppose he was quite clever. Nearly as clever as I was. But he was so… common!

That thick Galilean accent! Those rough hands and wiry muscles from all that manual labour! His father was only a carpenter, for heaven's sake! And my father—your grandfather—was the rabbi himself. The hours he spent with that boy… oh yes, everybody liked Jesus.

But not me. I saw through him, you see. I knew him for what he was—a troublemaker. And look how right I was!

But I was telling you about the trip to Jerusalem. Jesus had been going on and on about it to the point where I took him on one side and told him how childish it was to look forward to a religious festival so much. He just laughed. 'How can you be so calm about the Passover?' he asked me, with that dreamy look in his eyes. 'Don't you love Jerusalem, Jacob?' Well, love. Yes of course I love the holy city. It is my duty to love God's city. But to show this uninhibited glee at the prospect of going there… no, no. Most unbecoming in a boy of our age.

So we went and observed all the correct rituals for the Passover and did what was suitable in the temple and set off back home, our religious observance over for another year. The women and the brats went on ahead, while the men walked behind with us older boys who could be trusted to know what is appropriate behaviour. I was relieved when I noticed Jesus wasn't with us—his behaviour certainly could not be classed as appropriate. He still belonged with the little kiddies. I discoursed on

Leviticus, my favourite book.

It was only in the evening when the family groups got together for the night that I saw Mary talking to Joseph. She looked agitated, and I sidled closer, pretending to drink my soup, to hear what she was saying. 'I thought he was with you!' she said. And Joseph shook his head. 'I thought he was with you.' Well, really.

Jesus caused an immense upheaval, as we searched for him in every tent. A dreadful commotion. Mary kept saying, 'He wouldn't do anything wrong. Something terrible must have happened.' I put her right on that. To comfort her, you understand. 'I'm sure nothing terrible has happened,' I said. 'It is just Jesus' high spirits have led him into mischief. Again. It really is too bad, him upsetting us all like this.' Mary opened her mouth but nothing came out. Too shocked. I continued: 'He must be playing a silly practical joke and be hiding somewhere back in Jerusalem. I consider it my duty to return with you to look for him.' I would not take no for an answer, and, with my parents' approval, of course, the next day Mary, Joseph and I set off back to Jerusalem. They had little to say, so I soothed their spirits with quotations from the book of Proverbs about disobedient sons.

We split up to search Jerusalem. I went straight to the inns and houses of ill-repute, certain that he would have plumbed the depths of iniquity when he had given his parents the slip. But there was no sign of him. I decided to go to the temple and offer up a prayer. If his parents had lost Jesus for ever, I would pray for God's comfort in their loss. That was the right thing to do. They had other children, anyway.

But to my horror, there in the temple forecourt, surrounded by the most important teachers and thinkers of our age, was Jesus. The cheek! A boy! Wasting the time of all those learned men! I—I, the rabbi's son, would not have presumed to do such a thing. I thought he was just listening avidly as might have been proper. But then he asked a question—something about the Messiah—and I saw all the teachers pause, then start talking nineteen to the dozen all at once, as if they all had a new idea at the same instant. Most unbecoming behaviour. And it was all Jesus' fault. He'd wound them up.

Mary and Joseph were there already, watching. Mary waited for the teachers to pause for breath and then raised a hand to wave to Jesus. He jumped up at once and ran to her and hugged her, and she clutched him to her. I dashed up to hear what he had to say for himself. He didn't look remotely ashamed, as he should have been, just surprised. He said, 'Why did you have to look for me? Didn't you know I'd be in my Father's house?' You should have seen Joseph's expression.

We walked home, Jesus with his chin on his shoulder as he watched Jerusalem for as long as he could before the hills hid it from our view. I used the journey profitably to tell him exactly which rules he had broken by this shocking, inconsiderate behaviour, but I might as well have saved my breath. His eyes had a faraway look. Dreamer. Who did he think he was?

And look where his dreams brought him. Nailed to a cross in his precious Jerusalem yesterday afternoon. Well, that's the end of that rule-breaker. Keep the rules and you'll keep out of trouble. Like me. I was right all along.

5

Temptations

MATTHEW 4:1–11; MARK 1:12–13; LUKE 4:1–13

Matthew writes:

The Holy Spirit led Jesus into the desert, so that the devil could test him. After Jesus had gone without eating for forty days and nights, he was very hungry. Then the devil came to him and said, 'If you are God's Son, tell these stones to turn into bread.'

Jesus answered, 'The Scriptures say: "No one can live only on food. People need every word that God has spoken."'

Next, the devil took Jesus to the holy city and made him stand on the highest part of the temple. The devil said, 'If you are God's Son, jump off. The Scriptures say: "God will give his angels orders about you. They will catch you in their arms, and you won't hurt your feet on the stones."'

Jesus answered, 'The Scriptures also say, "Don't try to test the Lord your God!"'

Finally, the devil took Jesus up on a very high mountain and showed him all the kingdoms on earth and their power. The devil said to him, 'I will give all this to you, if you will bow down and worship me.'

Jesus answered, 'Go away Satan! The Scriptures say: "Worship the Lord your God and serve only him."'

Then the devil left Jesus, and angels came to help him.

Think of what you would most like in the whole wide world… What would you be prepared to do to get it? There are some athletes, for example, who are prepared to take drugs that change their whole bodies and even put their lives at risk if it means they will win a race. Is it always right to have what you want? Are scientists always right to perform experiments because they are able to? Do you know anybody who has said, 'I could do that, but I won't because I don't think it's right'? When did you last say that?

Jesus could have been any sort of super-hero that he wanted to be—the richest, the most powerful, the most admired man on earth. Why did he say 'no' to all those temptations?

Don't let him have it easy just 'cos he's God's Son.
Make him go through the worst like the rest of you have done.
Make him hunger, thirst, sweat and freeze,
Make him hurt like hell till he's down on his knees.

I'm talking 'bout degradation.

Get out to the desert, Jesus, have a change of scene:
Five weeks plus, by yourself, a sort of quarantine.
It's only then that we can see exactly what you're made of.
Let you fail your MOT and know that you're a write-off.

I'm talking 'bout isolation.

Forty days later, well, here comes I
Finishing a Mega-Mac with super-size fries.
Kick him while he's down. Make him lose his grip.
Lick that drip of ketchup from my lower lip.

I'm talking 'bout starvation.

'Are you hungry, Jesus, haven't you been fed?
If you really are God's Son, turn these stones into bread.'
It was easy that first time with the apple on the tree.
Once their stomachs rule them, they'll soon be ruled by me.

I'm talking 'bout temptation.

But this one didn't fall for it, he simply turned away.
'Don't live on food alone but on God's word, the Scriptures say.'
He dared to quote God's word to me, that shabby little man!
Well, if one can play at that game, then two definitely can.

I'm talking 'bout exaltation.

I picked him up, I took him high, the better to bring him low.
I took him to the temple's top, where only angels go.
Teetering on the parapet he trembled at the view.
'Jump!' I hissed. 'Let all men see his angels catching you.
I sense you're not quite certain that you are the Son of Love,
So put it to the test, lad, in the name of science—*prove!*
Prove you're God. Prove your power. Prove you are the best.'
He said to me, 'The Scriptures say, "Don't put God to the test."'

He's talking 'bout confrontation.

Reproduced with permission from *The Gospels unplugged* published by BRF 2002 (1 84101 243 2)

I winced at that, the second time he'd used the holy writ,
Slicing at me like a sword, he seemed a part of it.
As if the man and Holy Books were both one and the same
As if he and the Word of Truth were candle-wick and flame.

I stood well back and took a breath and tried my own best shot.
'Come see the glories of the earth—you know, there's quite a lot…'
I waved what passes for my arms, I showed the man the vista
Of all the wealth of all the world. No human could resist.
His starving gaze passed over the great hoards of Inca gold,
Of Indian spice, of Roman cities: 'Power and wealth untold,'
I whispered, struck with lust myself for all that priceless store.
'Bow down to me and I will give you more and more and more…'

'Bow down to you?' the human laughed. A man's strong laugh. 'Just go away!
"Worship God and serve him only." That's what Scriptures say.'

He's talking 'bout salvation.

He stood there safe from all my wiles, firm, a mighty rock.
Rooted, grounded, deeply dug—I crumpled at the shock
Of crashing headlong into him—the word of God slashed down,
Stabbing me with fire, to leave me screaming on the ground.
I writhed away to lick my wounds, soothe my bombarded senses.
Sticks and stones might break my bones but words can tumble princes.

I'm talking 'bout frustration.

You Living Word, you voice of God, you verb, you shout, you password,
You wait: you're only human now. We'll see who has the last word.

Reproduced with permission from *The Gospels unplugged* published by BRF 2002 (1 84101 243 2)

6

John the Baptist

MATTHEW 3:1–12; MARK 1:1–8; LUKE 3:1–20; JOHN 1:19–27

Luke writes:

At that time, God spoke to Zechariah's son John, who was living in the desert. So John went along the Jordan Valley, telling the people, 'Turn back to God and be baptized! Then your sins will be forgiven.' …

The crowds asked John, 'What should we do?'

John told them, 'If you have two coats, give one to someone who doesn't have any. If you have food, share it with someone else.' …

Some soldiers asked him, 'And what about us? What do we have to do?'

John told them, 'Don't force people to pay money to make you leave them alone. Be satisfied with your pay.'

Everyone became excited and wondered, 'Could John be the Messiah?'

John said, 'I am just baptizing with water. But someone more powerful is going to come, and I am not good enough even to untie his sandals. He will baptize you with the Holy Spirit and with fire.'

John the Baptizer—one of the most colourful characters of the New Testament! What a man! Who else do you know who isn't scared to point out injustice and try to put it right? And who do you know who never thinks about themselves but always points people towards someone more important? Do you think John ever got jealous of Jesus? (Look in John 3:25–30.) Do you know what happened to John the Baptist not long after this? (Look in Matthew 14:1–12.)

If you go down to the river today
You're sure of a big surprise.
If you go down to the river today
You'll probably be baptized...

I went to the river just to find out
What this crazy John the Baptist fever was about.
Soldiers like me have got better things to do
Than to hang around the desert with some batty guru.

Us soldiers, well, what can I say? We're mean and keen and tough.
We run a fair few rackets as we don't get paid enough.
You know—*'Just give us money or we'll tear your shop apart...'*
So I went down to the river with some crimes deep in my heart.

What was I expecting? Some nutter on the scrounge?
Some layabout or con-man with nothing to do but lounge
There in the sun and beg for gold? I've no time for that kind.
But what I found was someone who began to blow my mind.

There in the River Jordan stood this skinny, hairy bloke.
A crowd that sat around him hung on every word he spoke.
Spoke? He shouted! Bellowed! Hollered! Like my sergeant major!
And people whispered, 'Could this man be someone like Elijah?'

He frightened off the pompous jerks who'd only come to boast.
He called them 'snakes' and told the ones who had more than one coat
To give one to the poor, and share their food; be honest too.
I called down, 'And us soldiers? What are we supposed to do?'

Would he say, 'Just give up soldiering and follow me instead'?
I hoped he would, then I could simply laugh and shake my head
And turn away. But no. He thought. Then looked at me to say:
'Stop your protection rackets and be happy with your pay.'

His words made me step closer. Couldn't help it. I was driven.
'Turn back to God and be baptized! Your sins will be forgiven!'
He yelled. The people nodded, looked ashamed and bowed their head.
'Then get down to the water—get 'em washed away!' he said.

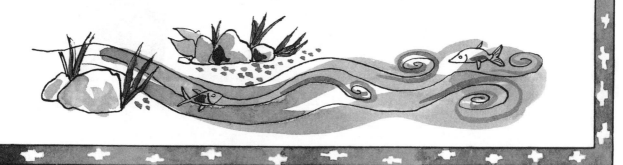

Reproduced with permission from *The Gospels unplugged* published by BRF 2002 (1 84101 243 2)

He seized each person, dunked them down, then brought them up again,
They were gasping, cold and dripping, but looked—well, it was strange—
Like an army fit for battle, like a bride ready to wed.
They were ready but not finished. 'What is going on?' I said.

I grabbed a dripping woman as she came up from the river.
Someone in silence passed a coat—they'd seen her start to shiver.
'Who is that man?' I asked her. 'A prophet? What's he made of?
What happens now? This baptism—what's it all in aid of?'

'If you want to build a road, then first you level out the land.
If you want to have a party, then you spring-clean beforehand.
If you want the star to shine, first warm up the crowd.
To give the seed a chance, then first the field must be ploughed.'

She smiled: 'John is the ploughman, he's the steam-roller, the cleaner.
He's just the support act. There's never been a
Man like him, and yet he claims that he is just the shadow
Of someone even greater and more holy who will follow.'

I stumbled to the riverside and felt my feet get wet.
I'd fought in battles but this was the scariest thing yet.
But John looked up and saw the gibbering wreck that I'd become.
'Don't be afraid. It's just the start. The best is yet to come.'

I wanted to get rid of all the guilt that weighed me down
So I let him push me under. Though it felt like I would drown
It was like the old me died and I'd been given a new start.
I was ready for action with a brand new clean heart.

And as I dripped my way back home, I thought about the one
Who would come next. An even greater man of God than John?
I'd watch for him and wait for him with purpose firm and steady.
I'm looking for this man of God. Thanks to John, I'm ready.

7

Calling the disciples

Or, The plaice of the sole in Christianity

MATTHEW 4:18–22; MARK 1:16–20; LUKE 5:1–11

Luke writes:

Jesus got into the boat that belonged to Simon and asked him to row it out a little way from the shore. The Jesus sat down in the boat to teach the crowd.

When Jesus had finished speaking, he told Simon, 'Row the boat out into the deep water and let your nets down to catch some fish.'

'Master,' Simon answered, 'we have worked hard all night long and have not caught a thing. But if you tell me to, I will let the nets down.' They did it and caught so many fish that their nets began ripping apart. Then they signalled for their partners in the other boat to come and help them. The men came, and together they filled the two boats so full that they both began to sink.

When Simon Peter saw this happen, he knelt down in front of Jesus and said, 'Lord, don't come near me! I am a sinner.' Peter and everyone with

him were completely surprised at all the fish they had caught. His partners James and John, the sons of Zebedee, were surprised too.

Jesus told Simon, 'Don't be afraid! From now on you will bring in people instead of fish.' The men pulled their boats up on the shore. Then they left everything and followed Jesus.

Jesus chose a range of people to be his special followers: his twelve disciples included political protestors, tax collectors and fishermen, but no princes, geniuses or prime ministers. Why did he choose such ordinary people? And what persuaded Simon Peter, Andrew, James and John to leave their fishing firm and go off with Jesus?

(By the way, I've taken artistic licence with the varieties of fish Peter talks about here. To the best of my knowledge, neither haddock, plaice, goldfish nor monkfish can be found in the Sea of Galilee, but who could resist rhyming God with cod?)

What a night! I'd a headache and arm-ache and cramp
And backache from working all night in the damp.
My hands were red raw from hauling the net
And my tunic was soaked with the waves and the sweat.
'Andrew!' I shouted, as we reached the shore.
'What was your catch like? I hope you got more
Than we did last night.' He shrugged. 'Not a sausage.
Not even a sardine to make me a sandwich.'

You win some, you lose some. But that night was bad.
The worst night of fishing that we'd ever had.
The crews were as grumpy as wintertime whales
As we shipped all the oars and we shook out the sails.
We let down the anchor and sploshed off to clean
The nets where our great catch of fish should have been.

And to our surprise, there on the sand
Was Jesus with huge crowds of people at hand.
'You're up early, Master,' I said with a grin.
'Have all of these come for their free medicine?'
'Eh, Simon! I'm so glad to see you,' he said.
'Can I talk to these folk from your boat there instead?
Just row me a little way out from the beach,
Then the crowd will hear every word that I preach.'
'You're on, Lord,' I said. 'Hop in and we'll row.
Just tell me how far you would like us to go.'
I thought that he smiled, and was going to say
Something important, not just 'Row away!'

Well, he talked and we lay in the warmth of the sun.
I tell you, that Jesus, he talked like no one
Had spoken before—it was like he knew God
Like the palm of his hand, like we fishers know cod,
Plaice, and haddock—that man knew his God inside-out.
In his stories he told us what life's all about.
And everyone groaned when Jesus had to say,
'Sorry, guys—that's your lot for today.'

He looked down at us as we lay in the prow.
'Thanks, Simon. I think what I'd better do now
Is pay you some rent—row your boat a bit farther,
Then let down your nets when we're out in deep water.'
Now he was a carpenter—we were all pros
At fishing. I frowned and I said, 'I suppose
You think you know more than the rest of us do?
We've fished all night, Master, and caught half a shoe!
There's not a fish out there, you take it from me.

You stick to your God-work, we'll stick to the sea.'
But he gave me a wink and a mischievous smile.
I sighed, 'Give him an inch and he'll send you a mile!
All right, Master, as it is you
We'll put down the nets like you told us to do.
But don't expect anything! Cast the nets, men!
Now watch and you'll see us catch nothing again...'

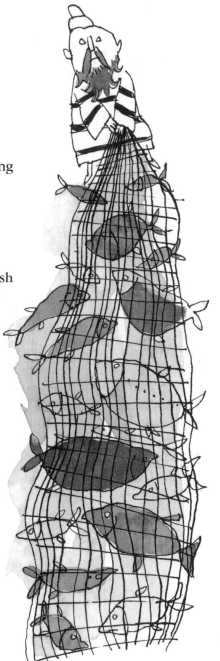

But my words faded out—we could hear a great thrashing
Of tails against scales, and we saw a huge splashing
From out in the nets, and the boat listed over.
'Heave, lads!' I yelled, then we all ducked for cover.
Each muscle was straining, each face drenched in sweat
From the weight of the thousands of fish in those nets.
There were oarfish and sawfish and swordfish and hogfish
And goldfish and flatfish and catfish and dogfish
And rockfish and codfish and jelly and trunkfish
And lionfish, stonefish and whitefish and monkfish.

'Andrew! Ahoy there! Bring out your crew!
And give us a hand—we need each one of you!'
We dragged in the nets, but what do you think?
There were so many fish, both boats started to sink!

I'd never seen anything like it before,
And I'd been at sea now for twelve years or more.
I don't mind admitting that I was scared stiff.
It was *unnatural*, it was as if
Jesus had ordered the fish where to swim
And the fish, against nature, had all obeyed him.

I fell to my knees; I was all of a panic,
And I said in a voice that was more than half manic,
'Stay back from me, Lord—I'm a sinful man.'
If he could do this—and I saw that he can—
What power he had! I was shaking with fear.
'Stop being afraid,' he said. 'Now listen here,
Forget about fish'—and I watched the lake ripple—*'I'm going to make you a fisher of people.'*

I looked at the catch piled high where it lay
And the fishing I'd loved seemed a lifetime away.
I forgot about plaice, didn't care about cod,
And I just looked at Jesus and knew he was God.
When we got to the shore I left my boat there.
From that day I followed Jesus everywhere.
Adventure and danger more vast than the sea
Were round every bend, after Jesus called me.

Reproduced with permission from *The Gospels unplugged* published by BRF 2002 (1 84101 243 2)

8

Wedding in Cana

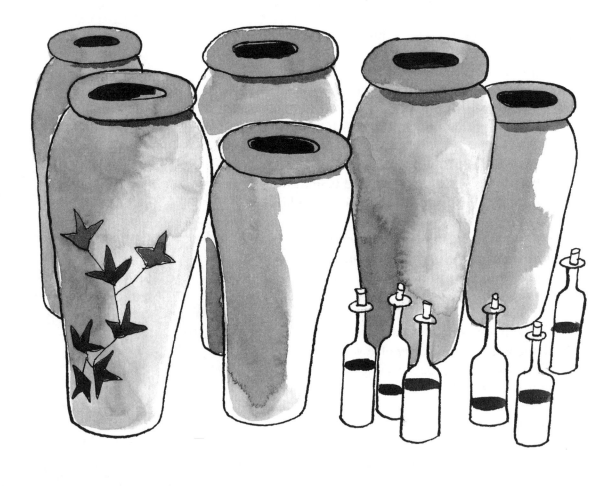

JOHN 2:1–12

Mary, the mother of Jesus, was at a wedding feast in the village of Cana in Galilee. Jesus and his disciples had also been invited and were there.

When the wine was all gone, Mary said to Jesus, 'They don't have any more wine.'

Jesus replied, 'Mother, my time hasn't yet come! You must not tell me what to do.'

Mary then said to the servants, 'Do whatever Jesus tells you to do.'

At the feast there were six stone water jars that were used by the people for washing themselves in the way that their religion said they must. Each jar held about a hundred litres. Jesus told the servants to fill them to the top with water. Then after the jars had been filled, he said, 'Now take some water and give it to the man in charge of the feast.'

The servants did as Jesus told them, and the man in charge drank some of the water that had now turned into wine. He did not know where the wine had come from, but the servants did. He called the bridegroom over and said, 'The best wine is always served first. Then after the guests have had plenty, the other wine is served. But you have kept the best until last!'

Changing water into wine, boring old water into the best-quality party juice—the first 'sign' of John's Gospel. What does this sign tell us about Jesus? Do you think that faith can change dull parts of people's lives and make them exciting?

Oh pants! Oh naff! We're out of booze!
What am I going to do?
There's ninety thirsty guests out there!
Hang on, guys, while I tear my hair
And chew my knuckles too.

I need a swig of wine myself!
Now, Sid, what is the matter?
Where are you off to with that huge jar?
Are you off your tree? You are!
You're filling it with water????

And Jane and Jess and Jim and Josh—
You're filling jars as well?
Is it just me that's going mad?
It must have been that pill I had.
Will somebody please tell

Me what is going on round here?
What? Jesus said to do it?
He's just a guest!
It's me knows best!
Bring back those jars! Jump to it!

Too late! The master's tasting it—
That water from your bottles.
Oh well, I'll kiss my job goodbye
I'll join the ranks of unemployed.
Hang on—he's drunk the lottle!

Get me a glassful. Goodness me,
That water's changed to wine!
Not sour and rough
But first-rate stuff—
Fruity, fabby, fine…

If Jesus pulls more stunts like this
Over the next few years,
Whoever he is,
Remember this—
The party started here!

Reproduced with permission from *The Gospels unplugged* published by BRF 2002 (1 84101 243 2)

The man with leprosy

MATTHEW 8:1–4; MARK 1:40–45; LUKE 5:12–14

Mark writes:

A man with leprosy came to Jesus and knelt down. He begged, 'You have the power to make me well, if only you wanted to.'

Jesus felt sorry for the man. So he put his hand on him and said, 'I want to! Now you are well.' At once the man's leprosy disappeared, and he was well.

Having leprosy in New Testament times meant that you couldn't lead a normal life with other people. You were cut off from society. You were untouchable. What sorts of people might be considered 'untouchable' or 'unapproachable' in our society? How do you think the man with leprosy felt when Jesus touched him? How can we 'reach out and touch' the cut-off people in our world?

Pretty sound, isn't it, my bell? Tingalingaling.

Spare a quid, sir? No? Oh well, can't blame him.

Yes, a very pretty sound. A touching little tinkle.

Trouble is, what it means isn't so pretty. Tingaling—don't touch. Tingaling—stay away, look out, here comes something nasty—me. You don't want to catch what I've got, do you? So tingaling—get out of reach. After all, I might reach out to you… Might even touch you… No, don't worry. I wouldn't do that.

As for you touching me…! Well, who'd want to? The doctor won't touch me. My family won't touch me. Even I look at what my hands have become and I get this shiver down my spine. I mean, look at them…

Oh sorry. Nearly forgot there for a moment. You're too far away to see, aren't you? And that's right. That's where you should be. Because if you came any nearer, you might catch this horrible disease too. And then… have you ever thought what it's like not to be able to use your hands? How would you catch a ball, hold a knife to cut up your food, hold a paintbrush to paint with? How would you hug the people you love? I used to hold my little boy's hand…

Spare a quid, madam? Sorry. Yes. I should have been ringing my bell. To warn you. To stay away.

It's like this disease has drawn an invisible line around me and no one dares cross it.

But have you heard there's a healer coming to town today? Jesus. From Nazareth. They say he's got great power. They say he does miracles. They say he makes people better from all kinds of illnesses. I shouldn't go near him, I know. But perhaps he could make me better. If he wanted to.

There he is, in the distance. What shall I do?

The paralysed man through the roof

A very holey story

(For the children at Stelling Minnis School)

MATTHEW 9:1–8; MARK 2:1–12; LUKE 5:17–26

Mark writes:

Jesus went back to Capernaum, and a few days later people heard that he was at home. Then so many of them came to the house that there wasn't even standing room left in front of the door.

Jesus was still teaching when four people came up, carrying a crippled man on a mat. But because of the crowd, they could not get him to Jesus. So they made a hole in the roof above him and let the man down in front of everyone.

When Jesus saw how much faith they had, he said to the crippled man, 'My friend, your sins are forgiven.'

Some of the teachers of the Law of Moses were sitting there. They started wondering, 'Why would he say such a thing? He must think he is God! Only God can forgive sins!'

Straight away, Jesus knew what they were thinking, and he said, 'Why are you thinking such things? Is it easier for me to tell this crippled man that his sins are forgiven or to tell him to pick up his mat and go on home? I will show you that the Son of Man has the right to forgive sins here on earth.' So Jesus said to the man, 'Get up! Pick up your mat and go on home.'

The man got straight up. He picked up his mat and went out while everyone watched in amazement. They praised God and said, 'We have never seen anything like this!'

What do the friends in this story do that proves what good friends they are? What do you think makes a good friend? Which do you think was more difficult for Jesus to do—to heal the man on the inside or the outside? Why do you think the Pharisees were muttering?

There we was, one summer's day, the five of us was sat.
Well, Josh, Jim, Joe and me were sitting—Ben lay on his mat.
We were happy in the wine bar, me and Josh, Jim, Ben and Joe,
Sorting out the nation's problems over sixteen pints or so,
When Joe pipes up, ''Ere lads, I knew I had something to say.
Did you know that Jesus bloke is here in town today?'

We looked at Ben, then at each other. Everyone knew what
Joe meant because Ben's legs, you see, were both completely shot.
They wouldn't move. They never had, just lay there like two sticks.
'Sometimes,' Ben says, 'life isn't fair, it really makes you sick.
I mean, why should a lad like me who's not done nothing wrong
Be born with two bad legs and be in pain his whole life long?'

And now it seemed that Joe had heard this Jesus was worth trying.
'They say he does great miracles!' we all heard Joseph crying.
'They say he heals the sick, they say he mends the broken! Ben!
Perhaps, *perhaps* he's got the power to make you walk again!'

'Oh yeah?' sneered Ben. 'And tell me, Joseph, what means should I try
To get up to this Jesus bloke—maybe I should fly?'
'You berk!' yelled Joe. 'There's four of us and only one of you!
Grab him, lads, we'll carry him! And pick his mat up too!'

Before young Ben could squawk 'Oh no!' we'd heaved him to our shoulders
And lugged him out the wine bar to the shock of the beholders.
'Which way?' gasped Jim. 'Let go!' wailed Ben. 'I'm feeling very seasick.'
Josh said, 'Cor Ben, you weigh a ton, for heaven's sake let's be quick!'
I said, 'Let's try the holy men, they'll know where Jesus is.'
But when we staggered to their house, Joe grunted, 'What a swizz.'
We couldn't get inside the house! Couldn't get him near it!
Someone said, 'Jesus is talking—we've all come to hear it.'
There were crowds of people round the front, and round the sides, still more.
Shoving heads in through the windows, pushing down the door.
I said, 'Reverse, lads! When have you seen crowds as big as these?
It's like at the cup final. How can we get through to Jesus?'
'Are you going to put me down?' yelled Ben from by my ear.
'Ah Ben, me lad,' I grinned at him. 'You gave me an idea.
Up on the roof with you, my boy. Come on, lads, up the stair.
Carry him up quickly, and now lay his mat out there.'
'Here, what is going on?' said Ben. 'I've got a nasty feeling…'
'Don't worry, Ben,' I smiled, 'we're going to shove you through the ceiling.'

While Ben lay back and groaned at us, the others got my drift
And we got out our penknives and we all began to lift
The plaster from the rooftop to make a whopping hole.
And we dragged poor Ben right up to it, him and his bedroll.

Reproduced with permission from *The Gospels unplugged* published by BRF 2002 (1 84101 243 2)

'Sssh,' I whispered, 'that's enough. Now knot your belts together
And we'll lower down the man and mat as lightly as a feather.'
'Oh no!' wailed Ben. 'Oh yes!' grinned Jim. 'Now he just needs centring...
I guess you realize that Ben is now breaking and entering?
Don't worry, Ben, we'll stand by you if you end up in court.'
'Oh thanks a bunch!' 'Now lower away! Keep those belt lines taut!
It's out of friendship we do this to let you meet with Jesus.'
'With friends like you,' hissed Ben, 'just tell me, who needs enemies?'

We took the strain; the mat broke through, the plaster showered down
On the staring upturned faces of the poshest men in town.
'Oh cripes,' I thought. 'What have we done? We've really got a nerve,
But if this bloke can heal our Ben, he'll get what he deserves.'
The mat and Ben fell with a bump and we looked down and gave
The thumbs-up sign, then Jesus looked right up at us and waved.

We waved right back and smiled at all the grumpy Pharisees,
And tried to show we're sorry but we had to get to Jesus.
'We know you'll heal our friend,' we called. 'Make him walk again!'
'This is so *embarrassing*,' we heard the sigh from Ben.
But Jesus said some words that could only offend
The Pharisees, and puzzle us. 'Your sins are forgiven, friend.'
Each one was shocked, and only we had time to see the change
In Ben; his frown turned to relief—I tell you, it was strange.
And while the people muttered: *'Only God can forgive sin!'*
We watched Ben's smile reflect the peace that welled up deep within.
Jesus asked them: 'What's the problem? Which is easier to say?
"Your sins, they are forgiven" or "Get up and walk away"?
But so you see I have the right to set you free from sin...'
He turned his back on all of them and only looked at Ben:
'Get up!' he said. 'Pick up your mat and walk home. Off you go.'
And silence fell as slowly Ben stood up and shouted *'Yo!*
Praise God! I'm standing! Look at me! My legs are good as new!
I'm jumping, dancing, praise to God! And thank you, Jesus, too!'

He pushed his way out through the crowd, striding down the lane.
And let me tell you, our mate Ben was not the same again.
But funnily, the fact that he could walk and dance and run
Was not the thing that made him different. What Jesus had done
Was set him free from fear, like a prisoner untied.
It was peace from sins forgiven that had changed him deep inside.

We still go out together for a night out on the town
But he's lost the bitterness that used to bring our mood right down.
And when he's danced us off our feet, he doesn't make a fuss.
It's not us carrying Ben home; it's him that carries us.

Reproduced with permission from *The Gospels unplugged* published by BRF 2002 (1 84101 243 2)

Healthy or sick?

The Pharisees get shirty

Later, Jesus went out and saw a tax collector named Levi sitting at the place for paying taxes. Jesus said to him, 'Come with me.' Levi left everything and went with Jesus.

In his home Levi gave a big dinner for Jesus. Many tax collectors and other guests were also there.

The Pharisees and some of their teachers of the Law of Moses grumbled to Jesus' disciples, 'Why do you eat and drink with those tax collectors and other sinners?'

Jesus answered, 'Healthy people don't need a doctor, but sick people do. I didn't come to invite good people to turn to God. I came to invite sinners.'

The Pharisees disapproved of Jesus and his friends—especially when Jesus started 'mixing with the wrong sort of people'. Why, do you think? Were they right to criticize? I chose a sonnet form for the Pharisees' grumble to the disciples, as its formality fits in nicely with their attitude that things are set in stone and can never be changed—especially not religion!

Ah! My good sirs! A word now, if you please.
Why are you at this party with this rabble?
You're shocking all us righteous Pharisees
By sharing food and wine from the same table!
To eat with someone means that you're their friend!
That you accept the loathsome things they do!
They're sinners! Wastrels! And I apprehend
If they're unclean, good sirs, then so are you!
And by the raucous laughter and wild chatter
It almost seems you're happy, at your ease!
Religion, sirs, is not a laughing matter!
You should avoid these sinners like disease!
But Christ said, 'It's the sick, not well folk, doctors see.
It's sinners, not the holy, who need me.'

Disciples

LUKE 6:12–16

About that time Jesus went off to a mountain to pray, and he spent the whole night there. The next morning he called his disciples together and chose twelve of them to be his apostles. One was Simon, and Jesus named him Peter. Another was Andrew, Peter's brother. There were also James, John, Philip, Bartholomew, Matthew, Thomas, and James the son of Alphaeus. The rest of the apostles were Simon, known as the Eager One, Jude, who was the son of James, and Judas Iscariot, who later betrayed Jesus.

Here's a rhyme to help you remember the names of the twelve disciples—and to remind us that the list of disciples can include such unlikely people as me and you! Matthew is another name for Levi, as seen in the piece before this one.

Bring on Simon Peter, a large and hairy lad!
And James and John, both brothers. (Zebedee's their dad.)
There's Andrew, Peter's brother, who is also into fishing,
And Philip and Bartholomew; it is astonishing
That Matthew's even on the list—'cos he's a tax collector.
Or Judas Iscariot, who turned out such a rotter.
There's Thomas (he's the scientist) and James son of Alphaeus
And Simon the Zealot, keenie-bean, and Judas (or Thaddaeus).
That's the lot, the twelve disciples, what a motley crew!
It's good to know that even I can follow Jesus too.

Love your enemies

MATTHEW 5:43–48; LUKE 6:27

Matthew writes:

Jesus continued, 'You have heard people say, "Love your neighbours and hate your enemies." But I tell you to love your enemies and pray for anyone who ill-treats you. Then you will be acting like your Father in heaven.'

People can think, say and do horrible things. Sometimes we need to admit that somebody has hurt us, either on purpose or by accident. Then we have a choice—we can either try to bury the feeling, or we can hurt them back, or there is a third way that Jesus opens up here.

Jesus knows all about how it feels to be hurt—people were trying to do him down as soon as he started doing his work. Can you think of times in the Gospels when people hurt Jesus, either on purpose or by accident? What does Jesus say we should do when someone's hurt us? Is it possible to do what Jesus teaches here? Does it work even if somebody really hurts us a lot? If we don't follow his teaching, how does hate hurt us? (And if you're being bullied, don't try to cope with it on your own—make sure a helpful adult knows what's going on.)

I want to kick them in the teeth! Slap them round the head!
Want to shake them till they're staggering! Stab them till they're dead!
They're mean to me, they're cruel to me, you've seen the things they do!
They bully me! They pick on me! Well, I hate them back too.

This loathing boils the heart of me, it eats me up inside.
It's a crazy wild stallion on which I choose to ride.
It's poisoning the way I live; I'm twisted with the stress.
I'm seeing red! I'm out for blood! I'll get my own back. Yes!

No! It needn't be this way. Give me a moment! Wait!
You're caught up in a spiral as the hate turns into hate.
A vile voracious virus—if you let it spread and spread,
Your enemies won't be the only ones who end up dead.

There is another way; it goes against what you've been told.
To break the chain, heal the wounds, turn rubbish into gold.
Here's the way to get control before hate devastates you:
Love your enemies; be good to everyone who hates you.

Put your neighbour first and put your needs in second place.
Offer them your other cheek if someone slaps your face.
Bless them if they curse you; if they're cruel, pray.
Give and give and give again. 'Impossible!' you say.

You can! You'll soak up hatred like a sponge that soaks up blood.
You're drawing in the evil and you're pouring out the good.
You're turning into profit what would otherwise be loss.
You're giving up yourself for them; you're carrying your cross.

Perfume

A Pharisee invited Jesus to have dinner with him. So Jesus went to the Pharisee's house and got ready to eat.

When a sinful woman in that town found out that Jesus was there, she bought an expensive bottle of perfume. Then she came and stood behind Jesus. She cried and started washing his feet with her tears and drying them with her hair. The woman kissed his feet and poured the perfume on them.

The Pharisee who had invited Jesus saw this and said to himself, 'If this man really were a prophet, he would know what kind of woman is touching him! He would know that she is a sinner!' …

Jesus turned towards the woman and said to Simon [the Pharisee], 'Have you noticed this woman? When I came into your home, you didn't give me any water so that I could wash my feet. But she has washed my feet with her tears and dried them with her hair. You didn't greet me with a kiss, but from the time I came in, she has not stopped kissing my feet. You didn't even pour olive oil on my head, but she has poured expensive perfume on my feet. So I tell you that all her sons are forgiven, and that is why she has shown great love. But anyone who has been forgiven for only a little will show only a little love.'

A hot country… no taps… no deodorant… few baths… it's safe to say that the New Testament world must have been a pretty smelly one by our standards. Perfume, especially the sort that was stored in alabaster jars, was mega-expensive. Perhaps the woman mentioned in Luke 7 had been keeping her precious bottle of perfume for a really special occasion. Then she met Jesus.

How does Jesus react to her 'over the top' actions? Look how tasteful and polite everything is until that moment. Is there a place for going 'over the top' in worship today? (You might like to read 2 Samuel 6:1–23.)

Here is a piece based on smells—have you ever tried to describe a smell in words? I found it really difficult.

A ghost of olive blossom stealing through the door on tiptoe.
Meeting, greeting, distant human oil of hair and skin and glands, salt sweat of a day's
work creeping through wool and linen,
Circulating discretely in the cool refined beige and chalk and magnolia space.
Stretching out apart, head towards the table, puff of armpit, legpit
Ignored under the stilted staccato of small talk,
Then beckoned by a swirl of spices, a pirouette of heat, a fandango of dancing dishes.
Slow waltz of the lentil stew,
Aerial ballet of saffron and coriander,
Tango of roasted goat with apricots,
Warm crusty bread tap-dancing.
Ah! So civilized. Each step closely choreographed.

But spurts of sophisticated scent as heads jerk up in shock
When a new dancer bursts on to the stage.
A raucous tawdry can-can of brash scent,
Not noticing the cosmopolitan cool.
Breathing only him.

Her reeking face meets his reeking feet
Until both bathe in a salty torrent of tears,
A tang of seaside brine.
Then plunge into the warm yeasty towel of her hair.
A gasp as the room explodes
In wave on wave of rainbow waterfalls of most precious perfume
Oil drawing in and breathing out no less than spikenard
Distilled by the most skilled, carried from the farthest by the bravest,
Sold to the richest, given to the most beloved, treasured for the greatest.

Other perfumes melt away, pale against its cloud of glory
Released by her?
Or him?

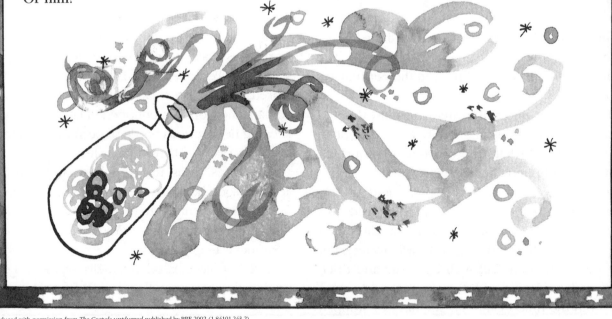

The sower

MATTHEW 13:1–9; MARK 4:1–9; LUKE 8:4–15

Mark writes:

Jesus used stories to teach many things, and this is part of what he taught:

'Now listen! A farmer went out to scatter seed in a field. While the farmer was scattering the seed, some of it fell along the road and was eaten by birds. Other seeds fell on thin, rocky ground and quickly started growing because the soil wasn't very deep. But when the sun came up, the plants were scorched and dried up, because they did not have enough roots. Some other seeds fell where thorn bushes grew up and choked out the plants. So they did not produce any grain. But a few seeds did fall on good ground where the plants grew and produced thirty or sixty or even a hundred times as much as was scattered.'

Then Jesus said, 'If you have ears, pay attention.'

Jesus knows that listening to God and doing what God wants are not always easy: look at how much of the seed in this story is wasted. But look how huge and fantastic the crop is from the seed that grows in good soil! A hundred times as much as was planted! God's kingdom begins in ways as tiny as a seed, and grows greater than we can begin to imagine. Which seed in the story would you choose to be?

This version of the parable is a vaguely musical one.

45

If you've got eyes, get seeing,
If you've got hands then do,
If you've got ears then listen,
This story's one for you.

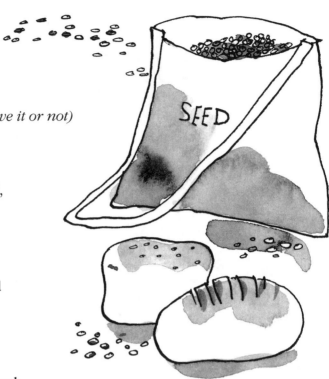

(To the tune of Old Macdonald, believe it or not)

Old Macdonald had a farm,
Ee-i-ee-i-o.
And on that farm he had some seed,
It was time to sow.

He poured the seed into his bag,
Took it to his field,
'Oo-arr,' he said, 'think of the bread
That all this seed will yield!'

And on that field there was a path,
Ee-i-ee-i-o.
He dropped some seed upon that path
But before it started to grow…

(To a bouncy beat)

There came a circus parade with fifteen elephants,
A troupe of ballerinas who all began to dance,
Thirty kids from Padnell* School in football boots and trainers
And half the Roman Army on their way to Venezuela…

As well as…

(To the tune of Sing a Song of Sixpence)

Four and twenty blackbirds, blue and red birds too,
Half a dozen ostrich escaped from London Zoo,
A flock of hungry seagulls, a budgie going tweet
And Old Macdonald's chickens who all wanted lots to eat.

And the seed on the path got…

(To a sad beat)

Trampled on and trodden on
And squidged and squelched and gobbled on
And pecked at and poked at and kicked off and squashed flat
Until it was all gone.

* or whatever school you like!

Reproduced with permission from *The Gospels unplugged* published by BRF 2002 (1 84101 243 2)

All together now… Aaah.

So Old Macdonald threw seed around,
Ee-i-ee-i-o.
And this seed fell on rocky ground
And this seed started to grow.

(To a rock beat)

'Cos it could rock (dum dum dum dum),
Oh yes it could rock (dum dum dum dum),
Threw down its roots and threw up its shoots
On the rock.
Stone the crows! Yeah!

(Sadly)

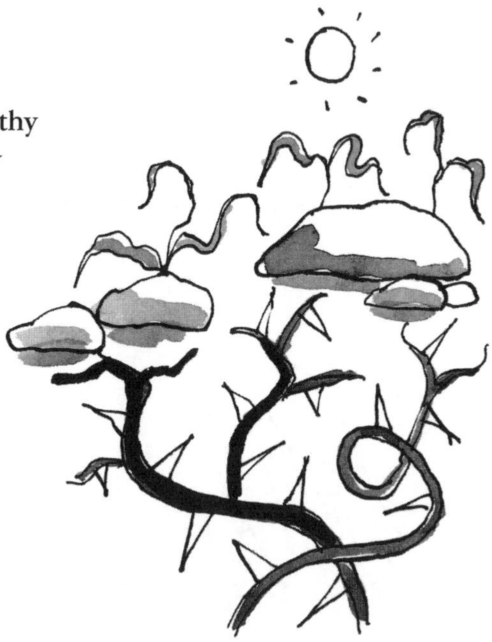

But it was dry on the rock and it wasn't very earthy
And the little tiny seedlings soon felt very thirsty
And one by one
They shrivelled up and died.

All together now… Aaaah.

So Old Macdonald sowed some more,
Ee-i-ee-i-o.
And this seed looked all right for sure,
Ee-i-ee-i-o.

But little did Old Macdonald know…

(Theme from 'Jaws')

That there in the ground already
(Jaws noise)
Were lurking the seeds of
(Jaws noise)
Thornbushes!!!!
(Jaws noise)
That grew up and strangled the poor little plants.
Urggggh!

All together now… Aaaaah.

Reproduced with permission from *The Gospels unplugged* published by BRF 2002 (1 84101 243 2)

(Very slow and tragically sad)

So Old Macdonald's seeds were sown,
Ee-i-ee-i-o.
And not a single one was grown…
Ee-i-just a mo…

Except…
The seeds that fell in the good ground!

(Very cheerily, to the tune of 'In An English Country Garden')

Strong healthy stalks and bushy shiny leaves
From the seed that fell on good ground.
Non-G.M., organic and resistant to disease,
The seed that fell in good ground.
Look at it! It grew and grew!
Miles of it, not just a few,
See it waving in the breeze!
There was flour for pies and poppadums and pancakes and for pasties
From the seed that fell in good ground.

Calming the storm

Sea sounds

MATTHEW 8:23–27; MARK 4:35–41; LUKE 8:22–25

Matthew writes:

After Jesus left in a boat with his disciples, a terrible storm suddenly struck the lake, and waves started splashing into their boat. Jesus was sound asleep, so the disciples went over to him and woke him up. They said, 'Lord, save us! We're going to drown!'

But Jesus replied, 'Why are you so afraid? You don't have much faith.' The he got up and ordered the wind and the waves to calm down. And everything was calm.

The men in the boat were amazed and said, 'Who is this? Even the wind and the waves obey him.'

There's a popular myth that becoming a follower of Jesus means life suddenly becomes easy. Peter and the other first disciples would have fallen around laughing to hear that. The new dimension to their lives meant they were thrown into situations that were scarier than they'd ever been in before. Do you know any stories about Christians who have suffered for their beliefs? Listen to the sounds in this account.

Eh, how the crowds yammer on and hammer on and gabble, babble, natter, chatter on, always just one more thing… Jesus! Just one more healing! Just one more story! Just one more miracle! Nag and beg and grab and nab from him, all day long…

'Let's cross the lake, lads,' he murmurs to us at last.

Hollow clop of sandals in the boat's bottom, snatches of sea shanties through our teeth.

'Keep it clean, Jimmy!'

Then squeak of ropes through pulleys, canvas lopping, leaping, flapping, cardboard thwack against the giggling breeze's shove.

Thud of bums on benches, grind of hull on sand and welcome lap and clap of water on the bows.

'Haul away, Andy!'

'Aye aye, Skipper.'

'Jim, watch your jib, there!'

'Teach your grandmother, Pete!'

'Now, lad, who's captain of this craft? Judas—don't touch that!'

Punch, guffaw, lads afloat—at ease at last, in our depth, on our lake whose every whisper is like a sister's kiss.

'Eh, Lord, I thought we'd never get away…'

'Phnourgh—pfffff, phnourgh—pfffffff…'

'Sssh—he's sleeping!'

'Reckon he's earned a nap. Gently with the mainsail, there.'

A silence a-buzz with contentment settles on the boat like a swarm of sleepy bees— rippling rills as the prow rips the satin sheet that sews itself behind us again with a playful slap. A piping thread of silver from a gull twisting in the billowing stuff of the sky. On every side a wide expanse of emptiness, our boat a single black note on watered silk.

'Skipper?'

'Aye?'

'See yonder?'

Hell's bells, John. It's going to be a… Get the mainsail down! Ship the oars! Batten down anything that moves!'

The swarm springs to life in a terrified buzz. Shouts from deck to mast. Creak and buffet as wood knocks on wood and sandals flap flap over the planks, palm's leathers slap timber and hemp.

'What's going on?' Matthew—a townie— never set foot in a boat in his life before he met us.

'Storm on the starboard bow, lad.'

'Starboard? You mean, port, Peter!'

'Fore!'

'Aft!'

Shouts from the sailors spin me round like a compass needle. Every way I look come galloping across the louring water the towers of clouds and roaring waves of storms, each one more massive than I've ever seen before. A grum growl of winds fulminates to a howl and shriek. From above, rainclouds thunder down on the boat. From beneath, water hisses in anticipation of the shock—

'Hold on, lads!'

Crash! Splinter! Groan!

Our boat moans and gasps with each kick, with each wall of water sluicing down in roars of outrage, bent on breaking us, sloshing us off our feet, calling us down down down.

Andrew shouting, can't hear him.

Matthew puking, John gasping. Judas shrieking. Phil, Bart, blubbering like babies. Thomas gaping at the forces savaging him.

Sailors hear what other men miss. And as the great waves suffocate the boat in smothering sheets, I could swear I hear from way down deep a booming, mocking laugh, and the roaring, searing wind seems to gloat aloud, *'Beat me.'*

A jarring crack of timber… a shift in balance…

'Peter! We've had it!'

Roars of anger now from me—

'Who brought us here? Whose fault is it anyway? What's that landlubber going to do about it? How can he sleep through this?'

Somehow I'm falling through the whips of rain and crashing down to thump him awake in sobs:

'Master! Wake up! Don't you care we're about to drown!'

His brown eyes open like shutters cranked slowly up.

As if on dry land, rises up to stand on steady feet on the bucking, shrieking, splintering raft, towering over us sailors splattered flattened on the deck. Closes eyes and listens to the spiteful whining of the air, vicious hissing of the water, thundering hubbub of mob defiance from every side.

His still small voice:

'That's enough. Be quiet.'

Water drops, swings, stills.

Wind drops, droops, calms.

And before we could peel ourselves up from the planks, to us:

'Don't you have any faith?'

The ripples bubble again. The gull sends her clear note shimmering down through the rinsed air. A whisper trickles round the dripping boat.

'Who is this man? Even the winds and waves do what he says.'

We sail on in a silence more scary than the storm.

Reproduced with permission from *The Gospels unplugged* published by BRF 2002 (1 84101 243 2)

Jairus' daughter

MATTHEW 9:18–26; MARK 5:21–43; LUKE 8:40–56

Luke writes:

Just then the man in charge of the Jewish meeting place came and knelt down in front of Jesus. His name was Jairus, and he begged Jesus to come to his home because his twelve-year-old child was dying. She was his only daughter…

While Jesus was speaking, someone came from Jairus' home and said, 'Your daughter has died! Why bother the teacher any more?'

When Jesus heard this, he told Jairus, 'Don't worry! Have faith, and your daughter will get well!'

Jesus went into the house, but he did not let anyone else go with him, except Peter, John, James, and the girl's father and mother. Everyone was crying and weeping for the girl. But Jesus said, 'The child isn't dead. She is just asleep.' The people laughed at him because they knew she was dead.

Jesus took hold of the girl's hand and said, 'Child, get up!' She came back to life and got straight up. Jesus told them to give her something to eat. Her parents were surprised, but Jesus ordered them not to tell anyone what had happened.

Can you imagine what it might be like to be about to die and then to be given your life back again? What difference might it make to the way you live? Do you think life is a present that we take for granted? What do you like about being alive? When do you feel most alive?

Do you know what my mates have been saying to me? 'You're only interested in one thing since yesterday. You've got a one-track mind!' And you know what? They're right!

I mean, they're interested in lots of things—what size earrings to wear, what colour dresses to put on, whether Tobias from the candlemaker's fancies Deborah or Miriam or Sarah… Oh, loads of things! But me, I've got a one-track mind!

Well, wouldn't you have if what happened to me yesterday happened to you too? Just wait while I pack this bag… there.

You see, yesterday I was dog-sick. I mean, sick as a parrot, sick as a one-legged camel in the middle of the desert. I just remember lying in bed getting hotter and hotter and thinking, 'If I get any hotter, my brain is going to burst out of my ears.' And then I don't remember anything. Which, after what they told me later, really racks me off, because it must have been dead weird.

When I woke up or… whatever… it was because there was someone calling me, like Mum does every morning. 'Come on, kiddo, time to get up.' But it wasn't Mum.

When I woke up… or whatever… there was this man standing next to my bed, holding my hand and grinning from ear to ear. Mum and Dad were right behind him, but they looked as if they'd seen a ghost. It was the man next to me who made me grin

back. He had the smiliest eyes I've ever seen—with little wrinkles round the edges like people have when they spend most of the time smiling. You could tell he was someone who just liked being alive, and wanted everyone else to like being alive too. He gave my hand one squeeze in his—big strong rough hands he had—and before I'd even jumped out of bed, we were both laughing. I wasn't hot any more: I felt weller than I'd ever felt before—aliver than ever.

Have you ever felt as if your whole life is ahead of you, as if you're about to step on to a rainbow? As if the whole world is waiting there like a present to be unwrapped? And suddenly I wanted to gobble up the whole world. I opened my mouth to tell him, but the man—Jesus, his name was—turned to my parents and said, 'She's hungry. I should give her something to eat.' Hungry? I was hungry for life!

They made such a fuss getting me a tray of food that Jesus went away before I could tell him. When I pushed my parents away and ran to the window and leant out to see him going down the road, I saw a funeral procession ready to begin. 'Who's died?' I asked Mum. 'You did,' she said.

Died? I can't die yet! I've got too much living to do first! And there's only one person who can show me how. Wait for me, Jesus, here I come!

Reproduced with permission from *The Gospels unplugged* published by BRF 2002 (1 84101 243 2)

18

Feeding five thousand

Rumbling tums

MATTHEW 14:13–21; MARK 6:30–44; LUKE 9:10–17; JOHN 6:1–14

John writes:

When Jesus saw the large crowd coming towards him, he asked Philip, 'Where will we get enough food to feed all these people?' He said this to test Philip, since he already knew what he was going to do.

Philip answered, 'Don't you know that it would take almost a year's wages just to buy only a little bread for each of these people?'

Andrew, the brother of Simon Peter, was one of the disciples. He spoke up and said, 'There is a boy here who has five small loaves of barley bread and two fish. But what good is that with all these people?'

The ground was covered with grass, and Jesus told his disciples to make everyone sit down. About five thousand men were in the crowd. Jesus took the bread in his hands and gave thanks to God. Then he passed the bread to the people, and he did the same with the fish, until everyone had plenty to eat.

The people ate all they wanted, and Jesus told his disciples to gather up the leftovers, so that nothing would be wasted. The disciples gathered them up and filled twelve large baskets with what was left over from the barley loaves.

After the people had seen Jesus perform this miracle, they began saying, 'This must be the Prophet who is to come into the world!'

One of the great things about God having lived as a human being is that he knows exactly what it feels like to be human—to be thirsty, hungry, lonely, sad, happy… And one of the great things about Jesus is that he didn't just care for people's souls, he cared for their bodies too.

Look how the boy gives what little he has and how Jesus turns it into something mind-bogglingly huge! What other stories do you know, from the Bible or elsewhere, in which something apparently tiny is made into something great? Would you trust Jesus with your tiny picnic?

You know that feeling you get
Like a twisting stripe of bright yellow in your tum
And it's kind of cold around it and you just know
Any moment now
It's going to give one almighty gurgling growl?

And the juices in your mouth start running
And the thoughts in your head start running
On juicy meat and crunchy vegetables
And sweet fruit and salt fish and tangy spice
And crusty bread and silky butter and sticky jam?

And the salt air blowing up from the shore sharpens your appetite like an axe-grinder
And you look at the grass under your feet and you wonder if it would taste so bad after all
And you realize you've been listening and laughing and marvelling and wondering full
blast since the morning and now it's tea-time and where did lunch-time go?
And it's a long way home.

But remember the bag on your back!
Fumble it open—secretly, as tums are rumbling all around now—what a feast!
Five rolls, a couple of fish should help fill the gap until you're home again.
Sneak behind a bush to guzzle in secret
But:

'Is there *any* food? Anything at all? However small?'
The rolls have little voices calling, 'Eat me! Eat me!'
The fish try to swim up to your open mouth.
You sigh and step out and shrug and say,
'Take this, mate. Take it all.'

Reproduced with permission from *The Gospels unplugged* published by BRF 2002 (1 84101 243 2)

They take you with them to the man
Who laughs away their rueful exclamations
And thanks you
And thanks God with full hands and open heart
And words that feed your soul
And breaks your bread and fish apart
And breaks it apart again

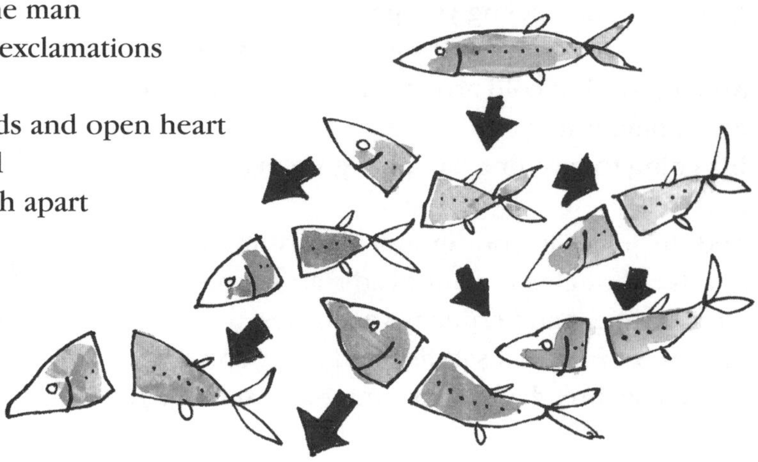

And again

And again

And…

Passing it on, giving it out, his hands darting through a shower of crumbs and laughing
in delight with the handfuls, armfuls, skirtfuls of bread and fish that his friends rush out
to the people, throwing it in great arcs of crusty crumby oily feasting.
You are standing in a sea of food, it is up to your neck, they can't pass it out fast
enough and you and the man are laughing at the sight of your heads poking through
the great heaps of fishy bits and chunks of bread.

You gaze at it—is it real?
You touch it, squeeze it, smell it,
Lick it, nibble it,
Munch it, gobble it,
Swallow it, wallow in it,
Roll in it, swim through it,
A whole mountainside of food!

You count the tubs of leftovers later.
When every one of the five thousand has
Gone away, stuffed to the brim:
Twelve, full to overflowing.

And all this from him.
And you.

Reproduced with permission from *The Gospels unplugged* published by BRF 2002 (1 84101 243 2)

19

Walking on water

MATTHEW 14:22–32; MARK 6:45–51; JOHN 6:1–14

Matthew writes:

Straight away, Jesus made his disciples get into a boat and start back across the lake. But he stayed until he had sent the crowds away. Then he went up on a mountain where he could be alone and pray. Later that evening, he was still there.

By this time the boat was a long way from the shore. It was going against the wind and was being tossed around by the waves.

A little while before morning, Jesus came walking on the water towards his disciples. When they saw him, they thought he was a ghost. They were terrified and started screaming.

At once, Jesus said to them, 'Don't worry! I am Jesus! Don't be afraid.'

Peter replied, 'Lord, if it is really you, tell me to come to you on the water.'

'Come on!' Jesus said. Peter then got out of the boat and started walking on the water towards him.

But when Peter saw how strong the wind was, he was afraid and started sinking. 'Save me, Lord!' he cried.

Straight away, Jesus reached out his hand. He helped Peter up and said, 'You don't have much faith. Why do you doubt?'

When Jesus and Peter got into the boat, the wind died down. The men in the boat worshipped Jesus and said, 'You really are the Son of God!'

Out of the three accounts of this story, only Matthew writes about Peter trying to walk to Jesus. I wonder if Peter was too embarrassed to tell Mark about his lack of faith when Mark was interviewing him for his Gospel. Why do you think the Gospel writers include stories that don't always show the disciples in a good light? As Peter may not have told anybody about it first-hand, I didn't feel it was fair to narrate the story from his point of view. So see how long it takes you to work out who's telling this story.

Can you rewrite the same story from yet another point of view? What would that person (or object, or animal…) see, hear, feel or understand?

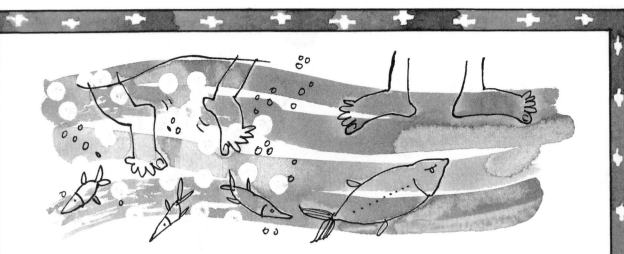

It happened one night in the darkest hour: four in the morning when the currents run cold and the wind whips the waves, the nadir of the night when the warmth of the day washed away hours ago and the dawn's light still lies deep buried under the horizon.

A lively time for us. A hide-and-seek time, a play-time, when the sea is ours and we can ride invisible through the rollercoaster waves. Hunters, we prowl the sea for food. We know every eddy; every chill and spill turns the school this way and that. There are rules for us and rules for the sea, and there have been since the dawn of time. Men trespass on to our territory, but they don't belong here. It is not their place. They can never control the dark power of the sea.

The howling wind kept all the boats at bay—but not that night.

We caught glimpses of the light up above through the drawing and withdrawing of the waves' curtains and, as from time before time, were drawn up to wallow in the light, to swallow the insects sucked by lantern and tension to the death-trap surface of the sea.

The usual walls of wood as the boat's bows bore down over us, easy to dodge in its sluggish plunging. No nets—not fishermen, then. Just travellers, too impatient to wait for the storm to abate. Would they join us down here? we wondered. We swam nearer, the bobbing lantern coating scales and tails and fins and gills with molten gold. Oh, rock us around in this wild sea—it's what we're made for, the tug and heave of forces too strong for us, that we can go with the flow, all in our elemental element.

Then, sensing as one mind something else. Something out of its element, more than the tossing, groaning boat above us. Something alien, incongruous, so wrong the whole sea shivered and protested.

There above us moved two light, fish-shaped, flesh-smelling feet firm and steady on the panicking water, padding not paddling, walking not wading. Held up against all the laws of the land and sea. We would have swum away but we were drawn to the feet as if they were another lantern: this was against the rules and if fish could scream we would have screamed with the men in the boat. The feet stopped and stood, laws unto themselves, not budging in the panting fury of the waves.

Beside the boat another foot touched the water. More men? Was this the end of our safe, savage world? Men dancing on our water and all the rules reversed?

But this foot sank, sucking the man down like a fly. Ankle, calf, thigh… We would wait until its thrashing pandemonium stopped and it sank, then we would follow it down to its final bed.

The firm feet stepped nearer. Words were spoken. The drowning man disappeared up out of our world. The feet vanished. The waves lowered to a lap against the sides of the retreating boat.

We swam down to the seabed, safe from the mystery of the world beyond.

20

Making the blind see

MARK 8:22–26

As Jesus and his disciples were going into Bethsaida, some people brought a blind man to him and begged him to touch the man. Jesus took him by the hand and led him out of the village, where he spat into the man's eyes. He placed his hands on the blind man and asked him if he could see anything. The man looked up and said, 'I see people, but they look like trees walking around.'

Once again Jesus placed his hands on the man's eyes, and this time the man stared. His eyes were healed, and he saw everything clearly. Jesus said to him, 'You may return home now, but don't go into the village.'

I can only begin to imagine what it is like to be blind. The blind man in this passage can only imagine what it is like to see. But he knows that something called 'sight' exists.

Perhaps there are senses apart from the normal five that we are not even aware of being disabled. In some people, the sense of spirituality is as dead as the blind man's sight is. They can only imagine a world that is gloriously obvious to others. Jesus was fully human, fully alive. What did he do to help others become fully alive too? What do his words mean to you: 'I have come so that you might have life, life in all its fullness'? What is a full life? Who do you know who leads the fullest life? Why is it full?

I see the world around me in seconds, not centimetres. The broken stone by my door is two heartbeats away. Five breaths beyond that is the first touch of the tree, brushing my face with its cool scented fingers. Another twelve taps of my stick and I can put out my hand and grate my palm on the knobbly width of its trunk, where I sit, warm but shaded from the dry heat of the sun.

The tree! They have told me its name (it only has one!), this contradiction of shapes—this frilled fluff of freshness and this unyielding rough tower which sends fragments of cool dampness down my fingernails. These savage weapons that stab, these creaking rustling expanses like wind in the ships down by the lakeside. A grounded ship, is it?

They said, 'A tree? It's a sort of pole with some green on top.'

Green? A growl to start it, a sharp acid middle to it, then the weak ending to it, this word: perhaps *green* sets your teeth on edge like rhubarb does? But the tree I see in the picture-book of my head is thick and delicate and tough and deep, not sharp. And huge like the sea, like the darkness, like the wind—it goes on and out and down and up as far as the ear can see.

There are no people in my world. There are voices that appear from nowhere, miracles of creation from nothing, springing full-grown from the silence. They make me jump. I have no warning of them. They cannot ease politely into my world with perspective. The best I can hope for is a word of greeting, clear enough to hear at the edge of my darkness but soft enough to give me time to recognize them.

Each person is a different shape, of course. Some are hands that help and guide and rest on me a moment in warm pretence of togetherness. Some people are all joints, clumsy, jagged, knocking and rushing. Some are clouds of love and gentleness; others are stones that fly past, smooth, sharp, unstoppable and unstopping. I know myself —the leather of my hands, the scaly ridges of my face, the dry coarseness of my hair. But other people? Their shapes, forms, size? They are aliens to me, living in a world of what they call sight, whatever that is, however that works. A world that is my world too, and yet a million heartbeats from mine.

Suppose, just suppose for a moment, that by some miracle I could see. That my eyes worked. That they filtered the world of images into my brain. Would my brain know what to do with them? How would it translate these objects, this new world that it has no names for, that it had learnt to recognize only through touch and smell and hearing? Would I know what is a tree? What is a person? I would be like a newborn baby. How many years would it take me to learn the same world that had become so totally different? The rest of my life?

I would need two miracles, not one.

Reproduced with permission from *The Gospels unplugged* published by BRF 2002 (1 84101 243 2)

21

The man born blind

The ballad of the blind man

JOHN 9:1–41

As Jesus walked along, he saw a man who had been blind since birth. Jesus' disciples asked, 'Teacher, why was this man born blind? Was it because he or his parents sinned?'

'No, it wasn't!' Jesus answered. 'But because of his blindness, you will see God perform a miracle for him. As long as it is day, we must do what the one who sent me wants me to do. When night comes, no one can work. While I am in the world, I am the light for the world.'

After Jesus said this, he spat on the ground. He made some mud and smeared it on the man's eyes. Then he said, 'Go and wash off the mud in Siloam Pool.' The man went and… when he had washed off the mud, he could see.

The man's neighbours and the people who had seen him begging wondered if he really could be the same man. Some of them said he was the same beggar, while others said he only looked like him. But he told them, 'I am that man.'

'Then how can you see?' they asked.

He answered, 'Someone named Jesus made some mud and smeared it on my eyes. He told me to go and wash it off in Siloam Pool. When I did, I could see.' …

The day when Jesus made the mud and healed the man was a Sabbath. So the people took the man to the Pharisees. They asked him how he was able to see, and he answered, 'Jesus made some mud and smeared it on my eyes. Then after I washed it off, I could see.'

Some of the Pharisees said, 'This man Jesus

doesn't come from God. If he did, he would not break the law of the Sabbath.'

Others asked, 'How could someone who is a sinner perform such a miracle?'

Since the Pharisees could not agree among themselves, they asked the man, 'What do you say about this one who healed your eyes?'

'He is a prophet!' the man told them.

But the Jewish leaders would not believe that the man had once been blind. They sent for his parents and asked them, 'Is this the son that you said was born blind? How can he now see?'

The man's parents answered, 'We are certain that he is our son, and we know that he was born blind. But we don't know how he got his sight or who gave it to him. Ask him! He is old enough to speak for himself.'

The man's parents said this because they were afraid of the Jewish leaders. The leaders had already agreed that no one was to have anything to do with anyone who said Jesus was the Messiah.

The leaders called the man back and said, 'Swear by God to tell the truth! We know that Jesus is a sinner.'

The man replied, 'I don't know if he is a sinner or not. All I know is that I used to be blind, but now I can see!'

'What did he do to you?' they asked. 'How did he heal your eyes?'

The man answered, 'I have already told you once, and you refused to listen. Why do you want me to tell you again? Do you also want to become his disciples?'

The leaders insulted the man and said, 'You are his follower! We are followers of Moses. We are sure that God spoke to Moses, but we don't even know where Jesus comes from.'

'How strange!' the man replied. 'He healed my eyes, and yet you don't know where he comes from. We know that God listens only to people who love and obey him. God doesn't listen to sinners. And this is the first time in history that anyone has ever given sight to someone born blind. Jesus could not do anything unless he came from God.'

The leaders told the man, 'You have been a sinner since the day you were born! Do you think you can teach us anything?' Then they said, 'You can never come back into any of our meeting places!'

When Jesus heard what had happened, he went and found the man. Then Jesus asked, 'Do you have faith in the Son of Man?'

He replied, 'Sir, if you will tell me who he is, I will put my faith in him.'

'You have already seen him,' Jesus answered, 'and right now he is talking with you.'

The man said, 'Lord, I put my faith in you!' Then he worshipped Jesus.

Jesus told him, 'I came to judge the people of this world. I am here to give sight to the blind and to make blind everyone who can see.'

When the Pharisees heard Jesus say this, they asked, 'Are we blind?'

Jesus answered, 'If you were blind, you would not be guilty. But now that you claim to see, you will keep on being guilty.'

This chapter of John is really funny and well worth a read—look at the ways the Pharisees try to wriggle out of admitting that Jesus did a miracle, and the blind man calmly repeating: 'I dunno—all I know is that I was blind and now I can see!'

How can people be 'blind' even when their eyes work perfectly well? Do you think it's just as much a miracle to make someone understand something new as it is to make a blind person see?

'A sinner all my life', they said,
A man born blind like me.
But there's one thing I know for sure:
Was blind but now I see!

One Sabbath day I heard a voice:
'Lord, why is this man blind?
Was it because he himself
Or both his parents sinned?'

The Lord said, 'Absolutely not!
But since he cannot see,
God will do a miracle.
Light for the dark, that's me.'

Without so much as, 'Do you mind?'
I heard a gurgly spit
And humming while he stirred the dust
And made some mud of it.

He slopped the muck on both my eyes
And said, 'OK, that's cool.
Now off you go and wash it off
In the Siloam Pool.'

As soon as all the goo had gone
I shouted 'Whoa! Yippee!'
No muddy dark before my eyes—
I found that I could see!

The people round about me said,
'Sorry we're nosey,
But you're the spit of a man we know…'
'The blind man? Yup! That's me!'

Reproduced with permission from *The Gospels unplugged* published by BRF 2002 (1 84101 243 2)

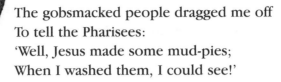

The gobsmacked people dragged me off
To tell the Pharisees:
'Well, Jesus made some mud-pies;
When I washed them, I could see!'

The Pharisees were most unchuffed.
'The Sabbath's not for healing!
This Jesus must be sinful
To commit a crime so chilling.'

'Um, 'scuse me,' said another.
'There's a little obstacle
To that idea, if we admit
This was a miracle.'

They squabbled back and forth a while
But they could not agree
If Jesus was a saint or sinner.
So at last they asked me.

I said, 'Jesus is a prophet.'
'What rubbish,' they replied.
They sent for Mum and Dad,
But poor old Mum was petrified.

'Dunno, your highness; sorry,
It's a mystery to me.
Yes, he was born bat-blind
And I don't know how he can see.'

'Swear that Jesus is a sinner,'
The Pharisees told me.
I sighed, 'Look, mates, all I know
Is that I now can see.'

'Tell the truth!' 'Again?' I cried.
'I've already told you!
Why should I shout it out again?
Are you his followers too?'

Well, it got nasty after that.
They hissed, 'Get lost, you dog.
And never dare set foot again
In any synagogue.'

I couldn't worship God at all!
The tears ran from my eyes.
But as I sat deep in despair,
To my immense surprise,

Jesus came to see me.
A sinner? Not to me!
'I'll worship you,' I said to him.
'Because you made me see.'

'I came to make the blind ones see;
To make the seeing blind.'
And eyes are more than in your face:
Your eyes are in your mind.

'A sinner all my life', they said,
A man born blind like me.
But there's one thing I know for sure:
Was blind but now I see!

Reproduced with permission from *The Gospels unplugged* published by BRF 2002 (1 84101 243 2)

22

Transfiguration

MATTHEW 17:1–13; MARK 9:2–8; LUKE 9:28–36

Mark writes:

Six days later Jesus took Peter, James, and John with him. They went up on a high mountain, where they could be alone. There in front of the disciples, Jesus was completely changed. And his clothes became much whiter than any bleach on earth could make them. Then Moses and Elijah were there talking with Jesus.

Peter said to Jesus, 'Teacher, it is good for us to be here! Let us make three shelters, one for you, one for Moses, and one for Elijah.' But Peter and the others were terribly frightened, and he did not know what he was talking about.

The shadow of a cloud passed over and covered them. From the cloud a voice said, 'This is my Son, and I love him. Listen to what he says!' At once the disciples looked around, but they saw only Jesus.

Peter, James and John, who saw Jesus meeting up with Moses (the law-giver) and Elijah (the prophet) from centuries ago, were gobsmacked themselves, as you might be if you saw a friend of yours meeting up with William the Conqueror and Julius Caesar. In this poem, Jesus stands on the hill halfway between one world and another. His God side sees that his mission is to die, but his human side needs reassurance.

Do you read me, Control? Do we have a link?
I'm high on a hill. I'm ready to listen.
And I think
I know my mission.

I long for home, for an end to trouble.
But here is where I belong as well…
Ah, Control, the strain of seeing double,
This dual nationality, amphibian life, can tell!

At stage one on the bank of the Jordan
You confirmed my choice to live for you
In this earthly limitation.
Now I understand stage two.

All the secret writings point to this,
The laws you set so long ago,
The coded future messages
Leave no doubt. But I'm human too!

You see, Control, living here, I know
What it is to be hurt, to fear, to be poor.
Life here hurts! *And yet*, life is so
Precious, before I give it up I need to be *sure*.

The planet and the people laugh with life,
Reflect your brightness like fragments of a mirror,
Surprises every second, beauty beyond belief.
Too much to throw away without being sure.

Send me the law-giver, for I cannot break the law.
Send me your interpreter too.
Let them beam down for a moment, no more.
Let me hear first-hand the other-worldly view.

And on the hill, between the far world and the near
The agents came and talked and yes, he was the one
To die. And clouds of glory fell, each droplet a tear.
Mission Control confirmed: *This is my chosen Son.*

Who is the greatest?

LUKE 9:46–48

Jesus' disciples were arguing about which one of them was the greatest. Jesus knew what they were thinking, and he had a child stand there beside him. Then he said to his disciples, 'When you welcome even a child because of me, you welcome me. And when you welcome me, you welcome the one who sent me. Whichever one of you is the most humble is the greatest.'

The disciples were squabbling about who was the top dog among them; who would deserve to be on top table at the banquet of heaven. Jesus knew they'd got hold of the wrong end of the stick. In Jesus' upside-down world, the person who puts themselves last and others first is the great one.

I don't know much, 'cos I'm not very bright.
I don't have a clue why stars come out at night.
I don't know how to read a book or tie up my shoelace
But I know one thing: I know my place.

My place is there behind the door, to hold it open wide
So that important people can walk easily inside.
My place is serving plates of food so hungry folk can eat.
My place is kneeling by them to wash their tired feet.

My place is listening quietly to every word they say
And taking in their sorrow and rejoicing in their joy.
My place is treating hurting wounds with olive oil and wine,
To hold the lamp to light their way before I light up mine.

My place, to hold a mirror up for other folk, not me,
My place is at the back to leave the better spaces free.
My place is standing in for them, my place to take the blame,
My place, I guess, could even be to give my life for them.

Reproduced with permission from *The Gospels unplugged* published by BRF 2002 (1 84101 243 2)

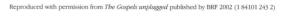

Good Samaritan Rap

(from The Mystery Tour)

LUKE 10:25–37

An expert in the Law of Moses stood up and asked Jesus a question to see what he would say. 'Teacher,' he asked, 'what must I do to have eternal life?'

Jesus answered, 'What is written in the Scriptures? How do you understand them?'

The man replied, 'The Scriptures say, "Love the Lord your God with all your heart, soul, strength, and mind." They also say, "Love your neighbours as much as you love yourself."'

Jesus said, 'You have given the right answer. If you do this, you will have eternal life.'

But the man wanted to show that he knew what he was talking about. So he asked Jesus, 'Who are my neighbours?'

Jesus replied: As a man was going down from Jerusalem to Jericho, robbers attacked him and grabbed everything he had. They beat him up and ran off, leaving him half dead.

A priest happened to be going down the same road. But when he saw the man, he walked by on the other side. Later a temple helper came to the same place. But when he saw the man who had been beaten up, he also went by on the other side.

A man from Samaria then came travelling along that road. When he saw the man, he felt sorry for him and went over to him. He treated his wounds with olive oil and wine and bandaged them. Then he put him on his own donkey and took him to an inn, where he took care of him. The next morning he gave the innkeeper two silver coins and said, 'Please take care of the man. If you spend more than this on him, I will pay you when I return.'

Then Jesus asked, 'Which one of these three people was a real neighbour to the man who was beaten up by robbers?'

The teacher answered, 'The one who showed pity.' Jesus said, 'Go and do the same!'

It's easy to forget the shock-value of this very familiar story. It's difficult to imagine the sharp intake of breath from the original listeners when they realized that this least likely of heroes outshone the Jews in compassion. Here it's some football fans who step across the dividing line of hate to show compassion. What other sorts of people can be as hostile to each other as the Leeds and Bradford fans in this rap? How brave do you have to be to 'cross over the road' and help a person you've been taught to hate?

This rap comes from a modern mystery play performed in Bradford Diocese—you might like to change the football teams to rival ones in your area.

Let us hit you with a story, man, we're feeling kinda hip,
And we'll tell you 'bout the girl who took her one mind-blowing trip.
The match was rough and Bradford City went in for the kill
But they lost away to Leeds. The score was (oh!) five–nil.

Five–nil? Oh no!

The crowds were mean, the crowds were wild, the crowds were getting mad
And what a time in keeping fans apart the coppers had.
Bradford hated Leeds and also vice versa.
In fact, I reckon Leeds United hated Bradford worser.

Go home! Get lost!

A Bradford fan was hitching home halfway across the moss.
Alone out on the moor road, but she didn't give a toss
Until a face loomed through the mist, which shouted, 'Hello sugar!
Your money or your life—I am your friendly local mugger!'

Mugger? Scary!

Mugged and beat-up there she lay with all her cash gone west
And not a stitch of clothing 'cept her knickers and her vest.
Our hero thought her number now was well and truly up
Till she heard the welcome 'brrrm–eee' of a car draw near and stop.

Save me!

Out leapt a girl, her coat was white, a stethoscope hung on her.
'Help me, doctor!' begged our lass. 'I reckon I'm a gonner.'
'Don't be absurd,' the doc replied. 'I've queues of folk to see.
I only stopped just here because I'm bursting for a pee.'

A second car drew to a halt. Great! Her own MP!
The one who fights in Whitehall for care in the community.
'If you'd let me in your Daimler, then my joy would be complete.'
'You must be joking. I don't want your blood upon my seat!'

Ow! Oooh! Feeling weak!

Will no one help? Will no kind person stop and ease her pains?
Half-dead, she heard a coach pull up, then terror filled her veins.
A coach of Leeds United fans, all young and full of beer!!
A Yorkshire voice belched twice and said, 'Now what do we have here?'

Help!

The end was nigh! Our hero gave up then all hope of life.
The best that she could hope for was a swift death by a knife.
She closed her eyes and crossed herself and broke out in a sweat.
The voice continued, 'It's OK, she hasn't pegged out yet.'

What?

'So heave her in the bus, lads, as fast as you are able.
Would you prefer Budweiser, Pils, or some Carling Black Label?
Drive on down to A and E, I think that would be super.
We'll get her in a private ward and pay the cost of BUPA.'

Super-dooper!

The Leeds United fans, they did exactly as they said.
They had her tucked up safely in a warm and comfy bed.
They brought her grapes, the *Yorkshire Post*, they even made her laugh
When they left her as a souvenir a Leeds United scarf!

Yeah!

Reproduced with permission from *The Gospels unplugged* published by BRF 2002 (1 84101 243 2)

25

Martha and Mary

LUKE 10:38–42

The Lord and his disciples were travelling along and came to a village. When they got there, a woman named Martha welcomed him into her home. She had a sister named Mary, who sat down in front of the Lord and was listening to what he said. Martha was worried about all that had to be done. Finally, she went to Jesus and said, 'Lord, doesn't it bother you that my sister has left me to do all the work by myself? Tell her to come and help me!'

The Lord answered, 'Martha, Martha! You are worried and upset about so many things, but only one thing is necessary. Mary has chosen what is best, and it will not be taken away from her.'

Most women I know sympathize with Martha in this story. It really does feel as if Jesus doesn't appreciate just how much work it takes to be hospitable! But did Martha really want to give him her best, or was she trying to show off what a good cook and cleaner she was? Do you think stuffing a mushroom is more important than listening to Jesus? How do we allow actions that seem very worthy to get in the way of listening to God? Do you think it's possible to do the things Christians are supposed to do without spending any time with Jesus?

Oooh I could slap my sister, the lazy so-and-so!
She never does a stroke of work; you think I'm joking? No!
And now we've got this guest—I know! It's nice of him to come
But all that blinking Mary does is sit there on her—

I've got all the work to do while Mary sits there chatting.
Oh flipping Nora! Can't she hear it? *Mary! Let the cat in!*
No? There, see? *You sit right there while I leave all my baking.*
After all, we wouldn't want your finger to start aching.

Up at dawn I was today, with all this work to do!
I've swept the house from top to toe and washed the curtains too.
Dusted, scrubbed and disinfected, every inch is pristine.
I don't think he's even noticed—and he calls himself a Christian!

And madam lounges at his feet, as happy as you please.
Oh, Mary dear, perhaps you'd come and grate this piece of cheese?
She hasn't even heard me! Sits there like a pig in clover!
Oh drat! Oh pooh! Oh bother! Now my gravy's boiled over!

Mary, any chance you'll come and clean up all this mess?
No? Never mind, I'll do it, we don't want to stain your dress,
Do we? Does she realize just how much work I do?
Stir the veggies, check the puddings, test the lentil stew…

Reproduced with permission from *The Gospels unplugged* published by BRF 2002 (1 84101 243 2)

Carve the radishes into those pretty little flowers.
Stuff the mushrooms—does he know that this takes hours and hours?
Can you lay the table, please? The plates are on the shelf...
I might have known, it's quicker just to do it all myself.

Crash the dishes down—I'm going to show them how I feel.
In fact, I'll say it! 'Lord, just look—it's me that's made this meal,
And Mary hasn't helped me when there's all this work to do!
You tell her off, get her to help, I know she'll obey you.'

And to my horror, he replies, 'Oh Martha, dearest friend,
You're in a tizz about so much, but really in the end,
The thing that matters isn't having loads of fancy sauces
But taking time to be together—who needs all these courses?

'So switch your cooker off, my love, and shut the kitchen door.
Let's bring out what you've made and we can picnic on the floor.
Give yourself and me and Mary one amazing treat—
And sit with us, you mean far more than anything we'll eat.'

Well, after all my tears and apologies were done
We picnicked in the way he said. It really was quite fun.
I said at last, 'And just to prove that I've learned what you mean,
I'm leaving all the washing-up. The cat can lick it clean.'

26

Prayer

MATTHEW 6:5–18; 7:7–11; LUKE 11:2–4, 9–13

Matthew writes:

Jesus continued: When you pray, don't be like those show-offs who love to stand up and pray in the meeting places and on the street corners. They do this just to look good. I can assure you that they already have their reward.

When you pray, go into a room alone and close the door. Pray to your Father in private. He knows what is done in private, and he will reward you.

When you pray, don't talk on and on as people do who don't know God. They think God likes to hear long prayers. Don't be like them. Your Father knows what you need before you ask.

You should pray like this:

Our Father in heaven,
help us to honour your name.
Come and set up your kingdom,
so that everyone on earth will obey you,
as you are obeyed in heaven.
Give us our food for today.
Forgive us for doing wrong, as we forgive others.
Keep us from being tempted and protect us from evil.

If you forgive others for the wrongs they do to you, your Father in heaven will forgive you. But if you don't forgive others, your Father will not forgive your sins.

Jesus continued: When you go without eating, don't try to look gloomy as those show-offs do when they go without eating. I can assure you that they already have their reward. Instead, comb your hair and wash your face. Then others won't know that you are going without eating. But your Father sees what is done in private, and he will reward you…

Ask, and you will receive. Search, and you will find. Knock, and the door will be opened for you. Everyone who asks will receive. Everyone who

searches will find. And the door will be opened for everyone who knocks. Would any of you give your hungry child a stone, if the child asked for some bread? Would you give your child a snake if the child asked for a fish? As bad as you are, you still know how to give good gifts to your children. But your heavenly Father is even more ready to give good things to people who ask.

If you flick through the Gospels, you'll notice there are lots of times when Jesus pops off on his own for a chat with God. It's as if he's a car filling up his petrol tank. Jesus' disciples asked him to teach them how to pray too. Here are two answers in two poems. Which answer do you think is Jesus' and who do you think might be giving the other one? Look at Matthew 6:5 if you're stuck. How are the two lots of teaching different? Can you find a famous prayer in this chapter of Matthew's Gospel? Why do you think Christians pray?

A crash course in prayer? I'd be glad to oblige.
You've come to the best, may I mention?
I've been praying for years and God is all ears.
When I pray, angels spring to attention.

First of all, make sure of crowds all around
To listen and gawp and admire,
Quivering and shivering as you are delivering
A holy and very long prayer.

For that is one secret, my ignorant friend:
Make prayers as long as you can.
Burble out jargon: let sentences drag on—
The signs of a great godly man.

Don't dare, though, to talk to our God like a father,
He couldn't be doing with that!
Keep it all formal; your words all abnormal,
Pronounced in tones boring and flat.

Fasting is good! If you go without food
The whole world will know you are saintly.
Let your gloominess show, let your grubbiness grow;
If you speak at all, let it be faintly.

Don't let anyone kid you that God wants to hear
The prayers of a sinful nobody
Like you. Even less is he ready to bless
You with answers to prayer—well, why should he?

So ask him for nothing. Expect no response.
Don't search for the answers, and when
You receive no reply, you won't wonder why.
That's the key to a prayer life. Amen.

Reproduced with permission from *The Gospels unplugged* published by BRF 2002 (1 84101 243 2)

When you pray, go to a room and shut the door behind you.
Keep it private, prayer's for you and God, can I remind you?
He knows what's done in secret and he can't wait to reward you.
So pray your prayer in private and be certain that he's heard you.

And when you pray (not *if* you pray!—prayer is just like breathing!)
Don't burble on for hours on end with words that have no meaning.
Before you open up your mouth, God knows all your needs!
So when praying, keep it simple. Say some words like these:

'Our Dad who is in heaven, we give honour to your name.
Come, set up your kingdom, so that it works the same
On earth as in your heaven, where what you want gets done.
We look to you to give us food, as you feed everyone.

'Forgive us when we do wrong things, exactly the same way
As we forgive the people who do wrong to us each day.
And help us not be tempted when we're choosing what to do.
And keep us safe from evil.' And listen to this too!

Though you're not perfect parents, all of you still know
How to give your kids good things—well, God is perfect, so
His gifts are brill! Go ask him, search for him, hammer on his door.
You will receive, you will find him, he'll open up for sure.

Reproduced with permission from *The Gospels unplugged* published by BRF 2002 (1 84101 243 2)

The Pharisee and the tax collector

LUKE 18:9–14

Jesus told a story to some people who thought they were better than others and who looked down on everyone else:

Two men went into the temple to pray. One was a Pharisee and the other a tax collector. The Pharisee stood over by himself and prayed, 'God, I thank you that I am not greedy, dishonest, and unfaithful in marriage like other people. And I am really glad that I am not like that tax collector over there. I go without eating for two days a week, and I give you one tenth of all I earn.'

The tax collector stood off at a distance and did not think he was good enough even to look up toward heaven. He was so sorry for what he had done that he pounded his chest and prayed, 'God, have pity on me! I am such a sinner.'

Then Jesus said, 'When the two men went home, it was the tax collector and not the Pharisee who was pleasing to God. If you put yourself above others, you will be put down. But if you humble yourself, you will be honoured.'

'Humble' is not a word that we use much these days. What does it mean? One of my favourite humble people is a lady called Betty. She firmly believes she is the least clever, the least holy and the least useful person in her church. But she's actually the person who's always there helping out, washing up, saying kind words, asking how you are, and putting other people first every single time. Who do you know who is humble?

Narrator:	Ever get the feeling as you read the local news
	That it's a great relief that you are simply you?
	That you're not like the people pictured in the paper—
	The criminal, the layabout, the anti-social leper?
Tutter 1:	How could he do a thing like this? The beast!
Tutter 2:	It's really grim!
Tutter 1:	And have you heard? He… *(whispers gossip too shocking to be shared out loud)* too!
Both:	I'm glad I'm not like him!
Narrator:	Jesus told a story of two men who went to pray.
	The first one stood and smiled a smile and then began to say:
Smug:	Oh God, I want to thank you that I'm not like other men.
	That I don't do the dreadful deeds daily done by them.
	Thanks that I'm not greedy or dishonest or unfair,
	That I'm not a total drop-out like that scumbag over there.
	How good I am! I fast each week although my tummy rumbles!
	I give so much to charity! Oh thank you I'm so humble!
Narrator:	The 'scumbag' on the other hand did not dare raise his head
	To heaven. He beat on his chest in anguish as he said:
Scumbag:	Oh God, have mercy on me. You know how sad I am
	That I'm a good-for-nothing scumbag and a really wicked man.
Tutter 1:	How dare he pray!
Tutter 2:	How dare he speak!
Tutter 1:	Or dare to think he can
	Set foot in here!
Tutter 1:	Oh, what a cheek!
Both:	You horrid little man!
Narrator:	But Jesus said, 'Hang on a mo—you might well think this odd:
	It was the scumbag, not the smug, who went home friends with God.

The rich fool

Shopping therapy

LUKE 12:13–21

A man in a crowd said to Jesus, 'Teacher, tell my brother to give me my share of what our father left us when he died.'

Jesus answered, 'Who gave me the right to settle arguments between you and your brother?'

Then he said to the crowd, 'Don't be greedy! Owning a lot of things won't make your life safe.'

So Jesus told them this story:

'A rich man's farm produced a big crop, and he said to himself, "What can I do? I don't have a place large enough to store everything."

'Later, he said, "Now I know what I'll do. I'll tear down my barns and build bigger ones, where I can store all my grain and other goods. Then I'll say to myself, 'You have stored up enough good things to last for years to come. Live it up! Eat, drink, and enjoy yourself.'"

'But God said to him, "You fool! Tonight you will die. Then who will get what you have stored up?"

'This is what happens to people who store up everything for themselves, but are poor in the sight of God.'

Jesus has a lot to say about the way we use our money. He knows what a powerful force the love of money is. So do the advertisers. Children and teenage customers are a major target for fashion firms. Which companies are getting rich from your money? And apart from money, what are you investing your energy in? Why do you think these activities are important? What are they worth 'if you die tonight'? What are your hopes, dreams and ambitions for your life? What do you think Jesus would think of those dreams?

Shopping therapy, that's for me!
Take me into town, set my Visa free.
Spend spend spend! Buy all I like.
My knickers are from Calvin Klein, my trainers are from Nike.
Designer girl, that's me me me,
My image is what the world will see see see.
    Red or Dead, 'swhat I said,
    French Connection, Fenwick, Benetton.
    Adidas, bold as brass,
    Slap their name across my sunglasses.
    Let me smell
    Of Chanel.
I want the world to tell tell tell
That I've got cash, that I look good.
I'll do what the TV says I should.
    Fill my wardrobe, fill my drawers
    With Next labels, because
    I am what I wear: that's what I've discovered.
No more room, better buy another cupboard.
Buy another wardrobe, fill it up with fashion,
Every essential essential for a season.
    Everyone knows it doesn't do
    To be seen twice in the same old shoes.
    Doc Martin,
    Dolcis, Caterpillar,
    Very very very very nice, at least until a
    Nother style comes along—I've run out of space.
Build another room to keep up the pace.
Never got enough! Always need more!
Throw all the carrier bags across the floor.
Pressure! Pressure! What'll I wear?
Build another house and keep my dresses there.
    No time to go out by the time I've chosen outfits,
    Mixed and matched my mobile phone and all my other gadgets.
Tomorrow I'll be trendiest, tomorrow I'll be best.
Tomorrow I will wow them in my Fat Face vest…
    Tomorrow
    Tomorrow
    Tomorrow
    All right.
        But what's your image worth if you die tonight?

Reproduced with permission from *The Gospels unplugged* published by BRF 2002 (1 84101 243 2)

Worry

MATTHEW 6:25–34; LUKE 12:22–34

Matthew writes:

Don't worry about having something to eat, drink, or wear. Isn't life more than food or clothing? Look at the birds in the sky! They don't plant or harvest. They don't even store grain in barns. Yet your Father in heaven takes care of them. Aren't you worth more than birds?

Can worry make you live longer? Why worry about clothes? Look how the wild flowers grow. They don't work hard to make their clothes. But I tell you that Solomon with all his wealth wasn't as well clothed as one of them. God gives such beauty to everything that grows in the fields, even though it is here today and thrown into a fire tomorrow. He will surely do even more for you! Why do you have such little faith?

Don't worry and ask yourselves, 'Will we have anything to eat? Will we have anything to drink? Will we have any clothes to wear?' Only people who don't know God are always worrying about such things. Your Father in heaven knows that you need all these. But more than anything else, put God's work first and do what he wants. Then the other things will be yours as well.

Don't worry about tomorrow. It will take care of itself. You have enough to worry about today.

Jesus owned nothing more than a set of clothes to wear, and yet he led the most fulfilled life anybody has ever lived. When he talks about not worrying about the things we need, he's talking from experience. Do you know anybody who takes these words seriously and who doesn't worry about money or clothes or food? What difference would it make to the world if we all lived out this teaching? Is it possible?

Where is your 'treasure'?

If I make it a command, will you take it seriously?
OK, then: *Do not worry.* That's meant unequivocally!
Don't worry about what you'll eat, about the clothes you'll wear.
Life's more than a burger or a scrunchie in your hair!

Look up there and see the crows! See them having fun!
They're soaring through the open air, wings spread to the sun.
Looping loops in lazy laughter, wafting where the wind blows,
Cawing out their raucous joy in simply being crows.

Do they plant corn? Do they hoard gold? Do they buy on Visas?
Do they spend hours worrying about their Peps and Isas?
Do they mortgage off their twiggy nests to satisfy their banks?
And yet God gives them food to spare without them having angst.

Can't you see, you harassed people, have none of you heard
That you are worth far more to God than any mere bird?
Can you make life last longer with all your worrying?
Why worry when your worry cannot change the smallest thing?

Look down there and see the flowers colouring the field.
Every petal, every bloom a miracle revealed.
Do they worry 'bout the clothes they wear? Do you see them stopping
Off to buy the latest styles? Do flowers go clothes-shopping?

And yet Dipsy and Po could not be half as brightly dressed.
The catwalks of Milan or Rome are only second best.
If God gives beauty such as this to mere wisps of hay,
Won't he do far more for you, day by day by day?

Don't worry about what you'll eat or what you'll have to drink!
It's only those who don't know God who cannot help but think
About such things. Your Father knows exactly what you need.
The rest will follow on if you allow God's work to lead.

Don't worry, little hassled flock! Don't panic, don't obsess!
Your Father wants to give you all his kingdom, no less!
Sell the things you have and give your money to the poor.
Keep your treasure treasured up in heaven where it's sure

To stay safe. Where no thieves can come and rob you of your gold,
Where it won't rust or melt away or else get all moth-holed.
A safe deposit, kept secure and treasured up for you.
For where your treasure is, you know, your heart will be there too.

Reproduced with permission from *The Gospels unplugged* published by BRF 2002 (1 84101 243 2)

30

The second coming

MATTHEW 24:45–51; MARK 13:32–37; LUKE 12:35–40

Matthew writes:

Who are faithful and wise servants? Who are the ones the master will put in charge of giving the other servants their food supplies at the proper time? Servants are fortunate if their master comes and finds them doing their job. You may be sure that a servant who is always faithful will be put in charge of everything the master owns. But suppose one of the servants thinks that the master won't return until late. Suppose that evil servant starts beating the other servants and eats and drinks with people who are drunk. If that happens, the master will come on a day and at a time when the servant least expects him. That servant will then be punished and thrown out with the ones who only pretended to serve their master. There they will cry and grit their teeth in pain.

The Bible promises us that Jesus will come back again. We think about this especially at Advent. No one knows when it will happen. It sounds scary! But if we're doing what we should be doing, it's actually something to look forward to—like the start of a party!

One picture Jesus uses to help us understand it is of servants waiting for their master to come home— are they ready and waiting for him or are they messing about, beating each other up, drinking all his beer and being sick in the flowerbeds?

Imagine for a moment that tomorrow you will be asked to explain everything you've done in your life. Is there anything you would like to put right before then? Anything on your conscience you would like to do something about?

THE MASTER

CERTIFICATE OF MERIT

Have you got your boots on?
Laces tied?
Are you wide awake,
Not slumped on your backside?
Has your torch got batteries?
So that it shines steady?
The boss is coming back soon!
Are you ready?

Are your eyes wide open,
Watching, waiting?
Is your house in order?
Are you concentrating?
Don't know when he's coming:
Could be late or early.
But the boss is coming back soon—
Are you ready?

What will he find you doing
When he bursts in like a thief?
Will his arrival be a shock
Or simply a relief?
What will he say about the way
You've treated everybody?
The boss is coming back soon.
Are you ready?

TOC
TIC
TOC
TIC
TOC
TIC
TOC
TIC

31

The cost

Large crowds were walking along with Jesus, when he turned and said:

You cannot be my disciple, unless you love me more than you love your father and mother, your wife and children, and your brothers and sisters. You cannot come with me unless you love me more than you love your own life.

You cannot be my disciple unless you carry your own cross and come with me.

Suppose one of you wants to build a tower. What is the first thing you will do? Won't you sit down and figure out how much it will cost and if you have enough money to pay for it? Otherwise, you will start building the tower, but not be able to finish. Then everyone who sees what is happening will laugh at you. They will say, 'You started building, but could not finish the job.'

Jesus wants people to follow him. But he also wants them to know what they are letting themselves in for. Someone said of becoming a Christian, 'Admission is free but the subscription will cost you everything.' The last time you started something but didn't finish it, why was that?

A board meeting of the company Juggins and Pratt plc

Juggins:	It will be a vision, I tell you! Hovering in outer space! The universe's first space hotel! Just off the second moon of Jupiter! The scientific accomplishment of a lifetime!
Pratt:	How big are we talking here?
Juggins:	We're talking three hundred miles from the anti-gravity play zone on one side to the Space Burger Bar on the other side.
Pratt:	That's big! And the design?
Juggins:	Oh, dig this design! I've brought in the hottest designers from around the world! We've got more planning behind this Space Hotel than there was behind the new Reception classroom *(or big local project)*! It will be staggeringly stunning! Superbly streamlined! Simply spiffing!
Pratt:	Super!
Juggins:	And luxury…! I've thought of everything! Built from base to roof in solid titanium… Triple jacuzzis in every room! Fifty restaurants catering for every cuisine around the globe… Everyone will be talking about it! We'll be the envy of hotel chains everywhere!
Berk:	Erm, hang on a minute…
Juggins:	Yes, every detail has been carefully planned out… The floors studded with semi-precious stones from across the continents… The doors inlaid with organic mahogany…
Berk:	The finances…
Juggins:	Window panes in individually crafted stained glass.
Berk:	Business plan?
Juggins:	Roof gardens!
Berk:	How much will…?
Juggins:	Nothing has been forgotten! And because I was so certain you would find this Space Hotel as thrilling a project as I do…
Berk:	Yes, but where are we going to find….
Juggins:	…the construction work has already started! As you can see on this webcam that links us to the Russian satellite orbiting Jupiter…
Pratt:	It must be at least five storeys high already! This is…
Juggins:	Ground-breaking!
Pratt:	This is…
Juggins:	Innovative!
Pratt:	This is…
Berk:	*Expensive!* How can we afford this? How much is this hotel going to *cost???*
Juggins:	Oh. The cost. I knew I'd forgotten something.

Reproduced with permission from *The Gospels unplugged* published by BRF 2002 (1 84101 243 2)

The great banquet

After Jesus had finished speaking, one of the guests said, 'The greatest blessing of all is to be at the banquet in God's kingdom!'

Jesus told him: A man once gave a great banquet and invited a lot of guests. When the banquet was ready, he sent a servant to tell the guests, 'Everything is ready! Please come.'

One guest after another started making excuses. The first one said, 'I bought some land, and I've got to look it over. Please excuse me.'

Another guest said, 'I bought five teams of oxen, and I need to try them out. Please excuse me.'

Still another guest said, 'I have just got married, and I can't be there.'

The servant told his master what happened, and the master became so angry that he said, 'Go as fast as you can to every street and alley in town! Bring in everyone who is poor or crippled or blind or lame.'

When the servant returned, he said, 'Master, I've done what you told me, and there is still plenty of room for more people.'

His master then told him, 'Go out along the back roads and lanes and make people come in, so that my house will be full.'

Choices… choices. You can't be born a Christian—you have to choose whether or not to accept your invitation to follow Jesus. What would you eat at your idea of a perfect party in heaven? How do you think the Jewish people who heard this story reacted to it?

Let's get cooking! Get it right! We're gonna have a party and it's tonight!
I sent out the invitations ages ago,
So you'd best remind them it's still on: off you go!
We'll decorate the house—get it bulging with balloons,
Streamers, party poppers. Find my favourite tunes
And test the mobile disco—sure it's loud enough?
And I'll check out the kitchen—wow, there's so much stuff!
Caviar and pickled onions, crisps and canapés,
Crunchy chunks of veggies you can dip in your satay.
Salads, sauces, joints of beef, a stonking great smoked salmon
And sandwiches without the crusts, with cheese and egg and ham on.
And puddings too! Huge éclairs with cream that's extra thick.
Trifles, pancakes, crème brulées, meringues and spotted dick,
Tarts and pies, profiteroles, sponges, jellies, mousses,
And as for drink—well, crates of wine and beer and fruity juices.
I'm dressed up to the nines and I can't wait for it to start!
My phone! What's this? You sound as though you've bad news to impart…
The guests won't come? You're kidding me! The party of the year
And they won't come? How can this be? Oh dear, oh dear, oh dear.
Now tell me straight, why won't they come? What did you discover?
I see. The first one's bought some land and needs to check it over.
The second one? He's bought an ox or two or three or four
And finds he must test-drive them. Oh right. Oh yeah. Oh sure.
And number three? Dare we hope we might expect him soon?
I see. He's just got married and has gone on honeymoon.
They didn't sound unhappy? Didn't sound apologetic?
They call those reasons not to come? I call them pathetic!
I'm hopping mad at every inadequate excuse,
But be it on their heads if they're determined to refuse.
Go off now to the streets and fetch me others to my bash.
Invite anyone you find there! Go on, you'd better dash!
We'll have a brilliant party with the lowest of the low,
And everyone who didn't come will all regret it so.
But if they change their minds, those who turned down my invitation,
Don't let them in. They've chosen to be out of the equation.
They had the choice. Their invitation given on a plate.
They had the chance to be my guests. But now it's just too late.

Reproduced with permission from *The Gospels unplugged* published by BRF 2002 (1 84101 243 2)

The lost sheep

MATTHEW 18:10–14; LUKE 15:1–7

Matthew writes:

Let me ask you this. What would you do if you had a hundred sheep and one of them wandered off? Wouldn't you leave the ninety-nine on the hillside and go and look for the one that had wandered away? I am sure that finding it would make you happier than having the ninety-nine that never wandered off. That's how it is with your Father in heaven. He doesn't want any of these little ones to be lost.

Look at the end of this story—in fact at the end of each of the 'lost and found' stories Jesus tells— each one ends with a party! What is being celebrated? What do you think an angels' party is like? (Check out Luke 15:10 if you think I'm making this up!)

Hey! I'm a shepherd with a collie and a crook.
You want to see my sheep? Well, there, take a look!
They're my pride and joy and just in case you wondered,
I know each sheep by name, yup, all a hundred.

There's Shane and there's Sharon and there's Cherie and there's Shula
And there's little Charlene with her fleece all soft and woolly
And there's Sheena and there's Sheila and there's Shirley the sheep—
I could count out every one but you just might fall asleep.

But stop a minute! Wait a moment! Have I got it wrong?
Has my maths gone crazy or has one sheep gone?
I thought I counted ninety-nine, this is most distressing.
Shaggy the sheep! Oh no! He's missing!!!

Get my helicopter with the big searchlight!
Call the Land–Sea Rescue! Find my fast quad bike!
Fetch the dogs! Call 999! Start my speedy jeep!
I'm going off to search for my little lost sheep.

Shaggy? Where are you? The night is very black.
And this cliff-face here is crumbling but I can't go back
Until I've found you, Shaggy. Oh no, the wolves are howling
And in the forest something really sinister is growling…

Thunder's rolling, winds are wailing and the lightning's flashing
And sheets of freezing sleet against my poor old back are lashing,
Where are you, Shaggy? Let me get you warm!
Let me get you home and sheltered from this scary soaking storm.

I've walked for miles, I ache with cold, I'm soaked right to the skin.
I can't give up until I get that Shaggy safely in.
My hands are frozen, I won't talk about my blistered feet.
Wait a minute. Did you hear that tiny frightened bleat?

Shaggy! I've found you! Was your fleece stuck in the bush?
I'll set you free and hug you tight. Calm down, Shaggy, shush.
There's no more danger, now, young sheep. Look! You're safe and sound.
I'll take you home. Then let's tell everybody that you're found.

Look everyone! I've found my sheep! Come party on with me!
Let's celebrate his safe return. Hooray, huzzah, yippee!
Oh Shaggy! Are you glad that you've been brought back from so far?
Shaggy simply looked at us and calmly answered, Baa.

The lost coin

LUKE 15:8–10

Jesus told the people another story:

What will a woman do if she has ten silver coins and loses one of them? Won't she light a lamp, sweep the floor, and look carefully until she finds it? Then she will call in her friends and neighbours and say, 'Let's celebrate! I've found the coin I lost.'

Jesus said, 'In the same way God's angels are happy when even one person turns to him.'

This is one of Jesus' stories told as a story game. To play it, sit everyone in a circle and give each person a name: Mrs Littlebottom, Mr Biggerbottom, 1p,

2p, 5p, 10p, 20p, 50p, £1 coin, big spotty hanky. You can have as many people for each name as necessary. As you tell the story, whenever anyone hears their name, they jump up, run round the circle and sit down again.

If you want to make the point that God loves us whatever our value, Mrs Littlebottom could lose the 1p coin instead of the £1 coin.

Once upon a time there was a lady called **Mrs Littlebottom**. **Mrs Littlebottom** was very poor. Being poor means you don't have very much money. But although she was poor, **Mrs Littlebottom** was usually very happy. To earn her living, she played her didgeridoo on a street corner and people threw money into her **big spotty hanky**. They threw in **1p**, **2p**, **5p**, **10p**, **20p** and **50p**. On really good days, someone might even throw in a **£1 coin**— then **Mrs Littlebottom** could have chocolate biscuits for tea instead of manky old digestives.

One day **Mrs Littlebottom** came home. She waved to her next-door neighbour, **Mr Biggerbottom**. And she went into her own house. **Mrs Littlebottom** was very happy. She had been playing her didgeridoo all day. And she had earned lots of money! One nice lady had even thrown a **£1 coin** into her **big spotty hanky**!

She emptied out her hanky on the table. The coins rolled everywhere! There was a **1p** and a **2p** and a **5p** and a **10p** and a **20p** and a **50p**.

'That's funny!' said **Mrs Littlebottom** to herself. Where's my **£1 coin**?

She looked and she looked through the pile of money. She found **50p** and **20p** and **10p** and **5p** and **2p** and **1p**, but she couldn't see the **£1 coin** anywhere.

'Oh dear, oh dear!' said **Mrs Littlebottom**. I must have dropped it when I emptied out my **big spotty hanky**.

So she began to search the room.

She looked under the table, but the **£1 coin** wasn't there.

She looked under the cupboard, but the **£1 coin** wasn't there either.

She got out her sweeping brush and swept every corner of the room, but the **£1 coin** wasn't there.

She was making so much noise, sweeping and weeping and wailing, that her neighbour, **Mr Biggerbottom** came to see what the matter was.

'I've lost my **£1 coin**!' wailed **Mrs Littlebottom**, throwing everything out of her cupboard, in case it was there.

'Never mind,' said **Mr Biggerbottom**. 'Look at all the coins you still have safe— there's a **20p** and a **10p** and a **5p** and a **2p** and a **1p** and a **50p**. That's lots of money!'

'But I want my **£1 coin**!' howled **Mrs Littlebottom** as she stuck her head up the chimney to see if it was there. She was so upset that she picked up the **big spotty hanky** to blow her nose… And out rolled the **£1 coin**!

'Look!' shouted **Mrs Littlebottom**. ' My **£1 coin**! Hooray! I've found it! Come on, **Mr Biggerbottom**! I'm so happy I could dance!'

And so **Mrs Littlebottom** and **Mr Biggerbottom** did a wild happy dance all round the **big spotty hanky**, and the **1p**, **2p**, **5p**, **10p**, **20p**, **50p** and the **£1 coin** all lived happily ever after.

Reproduced with permission from *The Gospels unplugged* published by BRF 2002 (1 84101 243 2)

The lost son

LUKE 15:11–32

Jesus also told them another story:

Once a man had two sons. The younger son said to his father, 'Give me my share of the property.' So the father divided his property between his two sons.

Not long after that, the younger son packed up everything he owned and left for a foreign country, where he wasted all his money in wild living. He had spent everything, when a bad famine spread through that whole land. Soon he had nothing to eat.

He went to work for a man in that country, and the man sent him out to take care of his pigs. He would have been glad to eat what the pigs were eating, but no one gave him a thing.

Finally, he came to his senses and said, 'My father's workers have plenty to eat, and here I am, starving to death! I will go to my father and say to him, "Father, I have sinned against God in heaven and against you. I am no longer good enough to be called your son. Treat me like one of your workers."'

The younger son got up and started back to his father. But when he was still a long way off, his father saw him and felt sorry for him. He ran to his son and hugged and kissed him.

The son said, 'Father, I have sinned against God in heaven and against you. I am no longer good enough to be called your son.'

But his father said to the servants, 'Hurry and bring the best clothes and put them on him. Give him a ring for his finger and sandals for his feet. Get the best calf and prepare it, so we can eat and celebrate. This son of mine was dead, but has now come back to life. He was lost and has now been found.' And they began to celebrate.

The elder son had been out in the field. But when he came near the house, he heard the music and dancing. So he called one of the servants over and asked, 'What's going on here?'

The servant answered, 'Your brother has come home safe and sound, and your father ordered us to kill the best calf.' The elder brother got so angry that he would not even go into the house.

His father came out and begged him to go in. But he said to his father, 'For years I have worked for you like a slave and have always obeyed you. But you have never even given me a little goat, so that I could give a dinner for my friends. This other son of yours wasted your money on prostitutes. And now that he has come home, you ordered the best calf to be killed for a feast.'

His father replied, 'My son, you are always with me, and everything I have is yours. But we should be glad and celebrate! Your brother was dead, but he is now alive. He was lost and has now been found.'

All through the Gospels we see how brilliant Jesus is at communication—getting his message across by using the best possible means to hand. If he were starting his work in the UK today, you can imagine him chatting to Lazarus on his mobile or sending Nicodemus e-mails. If the characters in one of his stories had today's technology, maybe the texting would have gone something like this.

Can you think of different ways in which Jesus communicated with people? In this story, what is he trying to communicate about how God feels when we do things that are wrong? There's an important part of the story that happens after the events touched on here—read it in the Bible and try to work out what Jesus is saying about how we should behave when people do wrong things and life seems unfair.

Sam, Pls Dnt Go.—Dad

Dad, 2L8! IOOH!—Sam

Ziggy, Hi Th M8! MunE$$$£££MunE :-) Im FrE! CUS.—Sam

Sam, :-) CU @ Kngs Hd 2Nite. Brng ££ LtsMkThsANIt2Rmba—Ziggy

Next day

Ziggy, WA Nite!! ;-) ;-)—Sam

Sam, Whr R U?—Dad

Dad, BZ @ TM—Sam

Next day

Sam, CU @ Qns Hd 2Nite. Brng ££££££££—Ziggy

Sam, Whr R U? MUSM—Dad

Dad, MYOB!—Sam

Next day

Sam, CU @ Cws Hd 2Nite. Brng £££££££££££££££££££££££££££££££££££££—Ziggy

Sam, Werv U bin? I Luv U—Dad

Dad, NOYB! LMA! :-(—Sam

Next day

Sam, CU @ Pgs Hd 2Nite. Brng Am Ex.—Ziggy

Sam, J2LUNILuvU—Dad

Dad! GL! :-((—Sam

Some time later

Ziggy, No £££ Lft :-(Cn U Lnd M £5?—Sam

Sam, BB. GL. UR So Sd. I H8 U—Ziggy

Ziggy, Spk 2 Me—Sam

Next day

Ziggy, Txt Me—Sam

Next day

Ziggy, Whr R U?—Sam

Next day

Ziggy!!! SOS!!! :-((((((((((((((((((((—Sam
Sam, RU OK?—Dad
Dad, Im So SRE. Cn I cm Hm? :'"-(—Sam
Sam!! :-)))))))))))))))) I CW 2 CU!! XXXX []⁣[]⁣[]⁣[] Lts PRT!! I Luv U!!—Dad

*

******************** Translation *********************

Sam, Please don't go—Dad
Dad, Too late! I'm out of here!—Sam
Ziggy, Hi there mate! Money, money, money! Hooray! I'm free! See you soon.—Sam
Sam, Great. See you at the King's Head tonight. Bring your money. Let's make this a night to remember.—Ziggy
Ziggy, What a night! Wink wink—Sam
Sam, Where are you?—Dad
Dad, Busy at the moment—Sam
Sam, See you at the Queen's Head tonight. Bring loads of money.—Ziggy
Sam, Where are you? Miss you so much.—Dad
Dad, Mind your own business.—Sam
Sam, See you at the Cow's Head tonight. Bring millions of pounds.—Ziggy
Sam, Where have you been? I love you.—Dad
Dad, None of your business! Leave me alone! I'm cross with you—Sam
Sam, See you at the Pig's Head tonight. Bring your American Express card.—Ziggy
Sam, Just to let you know I love you.—Dad
Dad, Get lost! I'm really fed up with you!—Sam
Ziggy, No money left. Oh dear. Can you lend me £5?—Sam
Sam, Bye bye. Get lost. You are so sad. I hate you.—Ziggy
Ziggy, Speak to me—Sam
Ziggy, Text me—Sam
Ziggy, Where are you?—Sam
Ziggy, Help!!! I'm really down in the dumps—Sam
Sam, Are you OK?—Dad
Dad, I'm so sorry. Can I come home?—Yours tearfully, Sam
Sam, Yippee! I can't wait to see you! Kisses, hugs. Let's party! I love you!!—Dad

Reproduced with permission from *The Gospels unplugged* published by BRF 2002 (1 84101 243 2)

I am...

JOHN 6:35; 8:12; 10:9; 10:14; 11:25; 13:46; 14:6; 15:1

Jesus refers to himself as 'I am' several times in the Gospel of John. This phrase has loud echoes of 'Yahweh'—'I Am Who I Am'—the most holy name for God in the Hebrew scriptures. Each of the 'I am' sayings paints a picture of who Jesus is, and they are loaded with symbolism. If Jesus was speaking today, what other 'I am' phrases might he use? We don't have many shepherds or vines around these days, in the UK at least.

Here are some kennings for the biblical ones, which unpack a little of their meaning. How many more can you write for each 'I am'?

I am the bread of life
Stomach-filler
Smile-maker
Nostril-filler
Life-giver

I am the light for the world
Blind-healer
Dark-destroyer
Crime-spotter
Eye-dazzler
Joy-bringer

Shadow-maker
Wound-searer
Path-lighter
Life-giver

I am the gate
Way-opener
Safe-keeper
Life-giver

I am the good shepherd
Name-knower
Wolf-fighter
Flock-leader
Life-giver

I am the resurrection
Death-defeater
Tear-wiper
Smile-bringer
Bright-painter
Hope-restorer
Future-guard
Candle-lighter
Life-giver

I am the way
Path-provider
Direction-maker
Destination-pointer
Home-bringer
Life-giver

I am the true vine
Sap-channel
Family-binder
Fruit-giver
Wine-provider
Identity-marker
Party-maker
Life-giver

Reproduced with permission from *The Gospels unplugged* published by BRF 2002 (1 84101 243 2)

Ten men with leprosy

LUKE 17:11–19

On his way to Jerusalem, Jesus went along the border between Samaria and Galilee. As he was going into a village, ten men with leprosy came toward him. They stood at a distance and shouted, 'Jesus, Master, have pity on us!'

Jesus looked at them and said, 'Go and show yourselves to the priests.'

On their way they were healed. When one of them discovered that he was healed, he came back, shouting praises to God. He bowed down at the feet of Jesus and thanked him. The man was from the country of Samaria.

Jesus asked, 'Weren't ten men healed? Where are the other nine? Why was this foreigner the only one who came back to thank God?' Then Jesus told the man, 'You may get up and go. Your faith has made you well.'

How fantastic to have been healed by Jesus! But most of these men he'd healed simply ran away, too excited to say 'thank you'. Only one took the trouble to go back to Jesus and say 'thank you' properly. But that meant that he was not only healed but had a special friendship with Jesus, too. Do you think Jesus was disappointed, puzzled or angry with the other nine? (It's interesting that the one who said 'thank you' was a Samaritan and the others were from God's special people.)

Think how many good things we take from God. Do we stop to say 'thank you', or do we just go the way of the nine men with leprosy—grab them and run? Which do you think is best—the gifts or the giver? When is it hard to remember to say 'thank you' to the people round us?

They must be completely bananas!
They must have all gone round the bend!
Being well makes you smile but it's better by miles
To have Jesus Christ as your friend.

We were hanging around on the edge of the town
Feeling spotty and scummy and sticky
When a man passed us by and we started to cry:
'Yo, Jesus, oh Master, have pity!'

He looked at us ten and he grimaced and then
He said, 'Go to the priests, 'cos you're healed.'
As we walked down the path we all started to laugh:
'I'm better!' 'Me too!' we all squealed.

I said, 'Let's give thanks,' but I drew quite a blank
As the others had run off, all joyous.
So all on my tod I sang praises to God
And galumphed at top speed back to Jesus.

The rest must have been raving bonkers!
They must have all gone round the bend!
Being well makes you smile but it's better by miles
To have Jesus Christ as your friend.

I fell at his feet and I said, 'What a treat!
You have made me all healthy and whole!
I'm so grateful to you, and to your great God too.
My thanks from the depths of my soul.'

Jesus said, 'And the rest? God gives of his best.
Are the other nine simply forgetful?
I healed all ten: what should I think when
Nine out of ten are ungrateful?'

But he beamed straight at me and I grinned back in glee,
And he said I was healed through my trust.
When I got up to go, I felt great top to toe,
In my body and soul I felt blessed.

The others don't know what they're missing.
They must have all gone round the bend!
Being well makes you smile but it's better by miles
To have Jesus Christ as your friend.

Reproduced with permission from *The Gospels unplugged* published by BRF 2002 (1 84101 243 2)

38

Blessing children

LUKE 18:15–17

Some people brought their little children for Jesus to bless. But when his disciples saw them doing this, they told the people to stop bothering him. So Jesus called the children over to him and said, 'Let the children come to me! Don't try to stop them. People who are like these children belong to God's kingdom. You will never get into God's kingdom unless you enter it like a child!'

Why on earth does Jesus say that we can't get into God's kingdom unless we go in like a child? What do you think children have got that adults often haven't? What adults do you know who really make time for children? Which adults do you know who are still like children in some ways? How? In Jesus' time, Jesus' behaviour here would have been very unusual, as children were considered much less important people than they are now.

I thought I had escaped them all!
Escaped their bossing, telling off.
Everything I do is wrong!
Nothing that I do's enough!
It's 'Stop it!' 'No! No!' all day long.
'Don't touch those! They're not for you!'
'Children should be seen, not heard.'
'Don't let me hear another word!'
'No! Not now! I'm busy! Shoo!'

I thought I had escaped them all
To play at kings by the olive trees.
And in my game I had the power
To run the world just as I pleased
For one long perfect summer hour.
But then I heard her angry shout:
'Where is that brat? Get down from there!
Wash your hands and comb your hair
And come with me. We're going out.'

'Where to, Mother?' 'Who asked you?
Who said that you could dare to speak?'
'I only asked…' 'Well don't. It's just
More of your naughty thoughtless cheek.
I suppose I'll tell you, if I must.

It's a rabbi that we're going to,
The one with power, oh yes, indeed,
And heaven knows, if anyone needs
A blessing, it's a brat like you.'

A rabbi! Another old, old man
Who'll mumble something to the men
And whitter on of things so boring—
Things that interest only them.
And I'll have to hide my yawning.
All this pointless endless chatter.
Teachers think they're so important—
They'll talk for hours to our parents
And say that children do not matter.

And this one seemed like all the rest
At first, in any case. We came
But his friends pushed us away,
Said it was a crying shame
To bother him—'Kids, run and play.
He's more important things to do.

'It's adults here, no kids allowed
You're too small. Come on, clear this crowd.
He's got no time for pests like you.'

But then the teacher, he looked up
From among the grown-ups where he'd been.
I saw his face, I watched it change
Through puzzlement, to fury, to calm again.
He knelt down and said something strange.
'Children, please come here to me.'
But as we waited, not quite sure
What his friends would do if we went towards
Him, he burst out angrily:

'Let the children come to me!
Don't try to stop them! Can't you see?
The kingdom of heaven belongs to those
Who are like children. Come to me.'
And I ducked from Mum and ran up close
To where he knelt upon the ground,
Holding out his arms and smiling.
Into his arms we all went piling
And it wasn't him that frowned.

There in his arms he whispered me
Secrets of the kingdom where I longed to be,
The kingdom of that summer day
Where God would sort things perfectly,
A kingdom where we'd shout and play.
But what he said out loud
To the grown-ups in the crowd
In a voice both strong and mild
Was this: 'You'll never get into
God's kingdom, unless you
Go into it like a child.'

Mum made me leave, and yet his words
Still flash like sunbursts in my head.
A kingdom where the king's my father,
A kingdom, as the rabbi said,
Where Dad and children play together.
Before I reach this heavenly home
I'll try to live my whole life through
As that rabbi would want me to.
And daily pray, 'Your kingdom come.'

Reproduced with permission from *The Gospels unplugged* published by BRF 2002 (1 84101 243 2)

39

Forgiveness

MATTHEW 18:21–35

Peter came up to the Lord and asked, 'How many times should I forgive someone who does something wrong to me? Is seven times enough?'

Jesus answered: Not just seven times, but seventy-seven times! This story will show you what the kingdom of heaven is like:

One day a king decided to call in his officials and ask them to give an account of what they owed him. As he was doing this, one official was brought in who owed him fifty million silver coins. But he didn't have any money to pay what he owed. The king ordered him to be sold, along with his wife and children and all he owned, in order to pay the debt.

The official got down on his knees and began begging, 'Have pity on me, and I will pay you back every penny I owe!' The king felt sorry for him and let him go free. He even told the official that he did not have to pay back the money.

As the official was leaving, he happened to meet another official, who owed him a hundred silver coins. So he grabbed the man by the throat. He started choking him and said, 'Pay me what you owe!'

The man got down on his knees and began begging, 'Have pity on me, and I will pay you back.' But the first official refused to have pity.

Instead, he went and had the other official put in jail until he could pay what he owed.

When some other officials found out what had happened, they felt sorry for the man who had been put in jail. Then they told the king what had happened. The king called the first official back in and said, 'You're an evil man! When you begged for mercy, I said you did not have to pay back a penny. Don't you think you should show pity to someone else, as I did to you?'

The king was so angry that he ordered the official to be tortured until he could pay back everything he owed. That is how my Father in heaven will treat you, if you don't forgive each of my followers with all your heart.

Forgiveness is one of those things that we expect other people to do to us, but we don't like doing to other people. Does that remind you of a line in a famous prayer? Jesus knows what a lot God has forgiven us, and tries to explain that what we have to forgive each other is, by comparison, a pifflingly tiny amount. In case you're worried about the torture at the end, don't be—it's a scenic detail in the parable to bring the story to life, not to imply that God has a set of thumbscrews.

In this account, Simon Peter is really racked off.

So I says to Jesus,

This lad outside the Fisherman's Rest—he'd
had too much to drink and just comes up
and punches me straight in the gut.
And I jumped up to teach him nobody
messes with Simon Peter.
But then I remembered what you'd said,
Lord, about forgiving other people the way
we'd like to be forgiven ourselves.
And I sat down again. I said, 'Hey hey—
that's OK. I forgive you, lad.'

And—you won't believe this, Lord, you
being a straight sort of bloke, but
he thumped me again!
And yes, I forgave him again.
And then…
He thumped me again! And again! And
again! And again!
And each time I said 'That's OK. Wiped out.
Forgotten.'

But then—you definitely won't hack this,
Lord—he did it again!!
Now seven times, Lord! That's more than
enough forgiveness.

That sort of forgiveness is saint level—
angel level—
And I'm no angel, I'm a fisherman. (Or I was.)

And Jesus laughs and biffs me on the back
and says,
'Peter—don't forgive someone seven times
over—'
And I think, bother, should have knocked
the lad for six in the first place—
And Jesus shakes his head and says,
'Not seven times but seventy-seven times!'
And falls about laughing.

I ask you.

And he wipes the tears from his eyes and
says,
'Listen, Pete—the kingdom of heaven works
like this:'
And I knew I was in for one of his stories
Where everything's upside-down and makes
more sense than anything on earth…
So I sat down on a rock with the rest of my
wine and nodded to him to get going.

'One day,' says Jesus, 'a king called in his
officials and asked them what they owed
him. One chap was brought in up to his
eyeballs in debt—he owed the king fifty
million!

'So the king says, "You can't pay that fifty million? Then you and your wife and your children will all be sold into slavery to pay that money back."

'The man fell to his knees and begged the king. "Have pity on me! I'll pay back every penny of the fifty million, I promise you, your majesty."

'And the king felt sorry for the man, and though he should have been sold into slavery along with his wife and children, the king let him go free—and let him off every penny of the fifty million debt.

'As he skipped out of the palace, the man met a friend of his who owed him a hundred pounds. The man grabbed his friend by the throat and started throttling him, shouting, "Where's my hundred quid? Pay me what you owe me!"

'His friend choked out: "Have pity on me! I'll pay you back the hundred I owe you!" But the man shook his head and had his friend slammed into jail until he could pay him back.

'The other officials felt sorry for the man's friend there in prison, and told the king what had happened. The king called the man back in and roared: "You nasty bit of work! When you begged for mercy, didn't I let you off your enormous debt? Why didn't you do the same for your friend?"

'The king was so angry, he ordered the man to be tortured until he could pay back everything he owed.'

And Jesus pokes me in the shoulder and says,
'That parable's to show you how my Father in heaven will treat you if you don't forgive each of my followers with all your heart.'
So I'm off back to the Fisherman's Rest.
And this time Jesus is coming with me—to show me how it's done.
Come on, Lord—it's nearly closing time…

Reproduced with permission from *The Gospels unplugged* published by BRF 2002 (1 84101 243 2)

40

Zacchaeus

LUKE 19:1–10

Jesus was going through Jericho, where a man named Zacchaeus lived. He was in charge of collecting taxes and was very rich. Jesus was heading his way, and Zacchaeus wanted to see what he was like. But Zacchaeus was a short man and could not see over the crowd. So he ran ahead and climbed up into a sycamore tree.

When Jesus got there, he looked up and said, 'Zacchaeus, hurry down! I want to stay with you today.' Zacchaeus hurried down and gladly welcomed Jesus.

Everyone who saw this started grumbling, 'This man Zacchaeus is a sinner! And Jesus is going home to eat with him.'

Later that day Zacchaeus stood up and said to the Lord, 'I will give half of my property to the poor. And I will now pay back four times as much to everyone I have ever cheated.'

Jesus said to Zacchaeus, 'Today you and your family have been saved, because you are a true son of Abraham. The Son of Man came to look for and to save people who are lost.'

Some of Jesus' actions are obviously miraculous—making blind people see again, walking on the water, turning a picnic into a meal for over five thousand people. But some of Jesus' miracles are less obvious. Would you say that changing someone's heart or turning someone's life in a totally different direction is a miracle? What do you think Zacchaeus might have done straight after this story? How do you think the people of Jericho would have reacted to him? Do you know anyone whose life has changed dramatically?

Ever felt that God can only love the people who
Are kind and nice and generous and tall and trendy too?
You feel that you're the only one who's not too hot at all,
You're nasty, mean and spiteful or you're ugly, fat or small?
'How could God love a jerk like me? He doesn't, that's for sure!'
Listen to my story, and you'll see how wrong you are.

The worstest man in Jericho was ultra-ultra bad:
A stinker and a rotter, a villain and a cad.
A traitor, thief, a criminal, a total reprobate,
Zacchaeus was the man that everybody loved to hate.
Zacchaeus was the tiny taxman, terror of the town,
Great men cringed before him and he'd look them up and down
(Well, actually more up than down, I suppose that it'll
Come as a big surprise to you—Zacchaeus was quite little).
Then he would cackle nastily and tot up every figure.
'You owe me lots, so pay up now and make my cash piles bigger!'

He'd tax the money from your wallet long before you'd spent it
And if the tax did not exist, Zacchaeus would invent it!
Tax on clothes and tax on food and tax on drink and betting,
Tax on walking, tax on smiling, even tax on sweating.
Tax on nose hair, tax on eyebrows, tax on earwaxes
And, if he thought of nothing else, he'd charge them tax on taxes.

'You nasty little man!' they'd shout. 'You've stolen this poor woman's
Last remaining copper coin to give it to the Romans.
You beastly little greedy shrimp, you vile collaborator,
We'll get you one day, just you wait, you and your calculator.'

Now one day, walking down the streets of that same Jericho
Came Jesus Christ, the Son of God, who was just passing through.
The crowds went wild! They loved that man! They wanted him to stay:
'Tell us stories! Heal our sick! Hip hip hip hooray!'

Zacchaeus heard the racket from behind his piles of cash.
'I'd like to see this teacher, so perhaps I'll make a dash
To see him quickly, then rush back to count my dosh again.'
But however much he nudged the crowd, he found it all in vain.

'Get lost, you squirt, go count your loot, go back and do your budget.
You're not standing in front of me, you horrid little midget.'
Zacchaeus was in deep despair. 'I only want to see!
I know! I'll get above the crowd, I'll climb this handy tree!'

Reproduced with permission from *The Gospels unplugged* published by BRF 2002 (1 84101 243 2)

And like a squirrel, up he shot and perched there like a budgie,
Clinging by his little legs—hairy, short and pudgy.
Above the crowd at first he saw the top of Jesus' head
And then his face, as Jesus looked up, grinned at him and said,
'Hello, Zacchaeus, come on down, have you got time for me?
I'd like to have a chat with you—can I come home for tea?'

The crowd was shocked and silent, and then some good person said,
'Don't you know that man's a crook? Come, eat with me instead.
It's dreadful that the Son of God should choose the vilest sinner
To go and waste his time with him and have to eat *his* dinner.'

Too late! Old Zac was on Cloud Nine and that was all because
At last he had met somebody who loved him as he was.
Jesus sat and talked and listened, ate his dinner too.
And then Zacchaeus knew that there was one more thing to do.
'Um, Jesus,' Zac said, after they had chatted half the night,
'I've been a real scumbag and I want to put things right.
You've made me see: of cash and people, people are worth more,
So I'll sell up half my property and give it to the poor.
And all those folk I've cheated, I'll pay each person back
Four times the sum of money that I stole from them in tax.'

And Jesus smiled and said, 'Zacchaeus, you have proved to me
You really have been saved, you and your family.
I came to find the lost and bring them back from far away
And that is the great miracle that's happened here today.'

So if you ever start to feel that you're the worst and wackiest
Of all your mates, just think about the story of old Zacchaeus.
Jesus loves you as you are: he wants to be your friend.
It's as easy (and as hard!) as that. So there we go. The End.

41

Limerick parables

(Just a bit of fun!)

Parable of the two sons

MATTHEW 21:28–32

Jesus said: I will tell you a story about a man who had two sons. Then you can tell me what you think. The father went to the elder son and said, 'Go and work in the vineyard today!' His son told him that he would not do it, but later he changed his mind and went. The man then told his younger son to go and work in the vineyard. The boy said he would, but he didn't go. Which one of the sons obeyed his father?

'The elder one,' the chief priests and leaders answered.

'Don and Dan, help me out!' their Dad puffed.
Don said, 'OK!' Daniel just huffed.
But they both changed their mind—
Dan helped; Don stayed behind.
With which was the father best chuffed?

Parable of the talents

MATTHEW 25:14–30; LUKE 19:11–26

Matthew writes:

The kingdom is also like what happened when a man went away and put his three servants in charge of all he owned. The man knew what each servant could do. So he handed five thousand coins to the first servant, two thousand to the second, and one thousand to the third. Then he left the country.

As soon as the man had gone, the servant with the five thousand coins used them to earn five thousand more. The servant who had two thousand coins did the same with his money and earned two thousand more. But the servant with one thousand coins dug a hole and hid his master's money in the ground.

Some time later the master of those servants returned. He called them in and asked what they had done with his money. The servant who had been given five thousand coins brought them in with the five thousand that he had earned. He said, 'Sir, you gave me five thousand coins, and I have earned five thousand more.'

'Wonderful!' his master replied. 'You are a good and faithful servant. I left you in charge of only a little, but now I will put you in charge of much more. Come and share in my happiness!'

Next, the servant who had been given two thousand coins came in and said, 'Sir, you gave me two thousand coins, and I have earned two thousand more.'

'Wonderful!' his master replied. 'You are a good and faithful servant. I left you in charge of only a little, but now I will put you in charge of much more. Come and share in my happiness!'

The servant who had been given one thousand coins then came in and said, 'Sir, I know that you are hard to get along with. You harvest what you don't plant and gather crops where you haven't scattered seed. I was frightened and went out and hid your money in the ground. Here is every single coin!'

The master of the servant told him, 'You are lazy and good-for-nothing! You know that I harvest what I don't plant and gather crops where I haven't scattered seed. You could have at least put my money in the bank, so that I could have earned interest on it.'

Then the master said, 'Now your money will be taken away and given to the servant with ten thousand coins! Everyone who has something will be given more, and they will have more than enough. But everything will be taken from those who don't have anything. You are a worthless servant, and you will be thrown out into the dark where people will cry and grit their teeth in pain.'

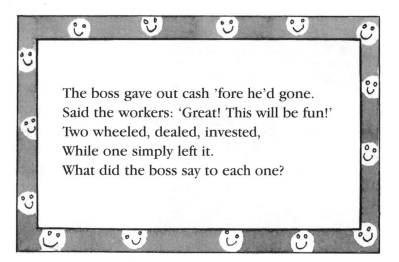

The boss gave out cash 'fore he'd gone.
Said the workers: 'Great! This will be fun!'
Two wheeled, dealed, invested,
While one simply left it.
What did the boss say to each one?

Parable of the treasure

MATTHEW 13:44

The kingdom of heaven is like what happens when someone finds treasure hidden in a field and buries it again. A person like that is happy and goes and sells everything in order to buy that field.

Said George, 'Who on earth would've thought it?
I have hunted and hankered and sought it—
And in this field I've found
Treasure! Under the ground!
So I've sold all I had and I've bought it!'

Parable of the two houses

MATTHEW 7:24–27; LUKE 6:46–49

Matthew writes:

Anyone who hears and obeys these teachings of mine is like a wise person who built a house on solid rock. Rain poured down, rivers flooded, and winds beat against that house. But it did not fall, because it was built on solid rock.

Anyone who hears my teachings and doesn't obey them is like a foolish person who built a house on sand. The rain poured down, the rivers flooded, and the winds blew and beat against that house. Finally, it fell with a crash.

One house with foundations dug squarely
And one house built all willy-nilly.
When the storms came along
The first house stood strong
But the second collapsed like a jelly!

Entry into Jerusalem

LUKE 19:28–38

When Jesus had finished saying all this, he went on towards Jerusalem. As he was getting near Bethphage and Bethany on the Mount of Olives, he sent two of his disciples on ahead. He told them, 'Go into the next village, where you will find a young donkey that has never been ridden. Untie the donkey and bring it here. If anyone asks why you are doing that, just say, "The Lord needs it."'

They went off and found everything just as Jesus had said. While they were untying the donkey, its owners asked, 'Why are you doing that?'

They answered, 'The Lord needs it.'

Then they led the donkey to Jesus. They put some of their clothes on its back and helped Jesus get on. And as he rode along, the people spread clothes on the road in front of him. When Jesus was setting off down the Mount of Olives, his large crowd of disciples were happy and praised God because of all the miracles they had seen. They shouted, 'Blessed is the king who comes in the name of the Lord! Peace in heaven and glory to God.'

The Jewish people wanted a Messiah, God's Chosen One (like Neo in the film of *The Matrix*), to save them from the Roman army which was occupying their country. But Jesus wasn't there to set up a political kingdom. He'd decided that, right back in the desert when the devil tempted him. What kingdom was Jesus bringing to Jerusalem?

Stone the Romans! That's the game! It keeps them on their toes.
My pebble hit! Oh yes! It caught the soldier on the nose!
I sniggered as I heard his 'Ouch! Those Jewish kids! Cor blimey!'
Then I scuttled right away so there was no chance he would spy me.

I ran like crazy down the streets, my heart was beating hard
And I skittered, safe and sound at last, right into our back yard.
But what I saw there stopped me dead. Two men were there already.
Those burglars were taking off my favourite donkey, Neddy!

I shouted, 'You joyriders, where do you think you're going?
You let my donkey go, you crooks—what do you think you're doing?'
I ran and grabbed him: 'Hands off, guys! This donkey's ours, not yours!'
And Neddy, bless him, lifts his head and lets out three eeyores.

Then out comes Dad to sort it all, much to my relief,
I've never had to deal before with any donkey thief.
The men just shrugged and grinned at Dad, and said, 'You'd best believe it:
We were told to tell you simply: the Lord needs it.'

To my amazement, Dad did not put up the least resistance.
'Then take the beast! I'm proud that we can be of such assistance.'
I said, 'But, Dad…!' He took me by the arm and shook his head.
The two men thanked him, then they led away our little Ned.

'You follow if you want, my boy,' he laughed. 'You'll never see a
Nother sight so marvellous all across Judea.
Rome has had it this time! Drop those occupation blues!
Long live the Revolution! It's freedom for the Jews!'

Freedom from the Romans? What was Dad on about?
And how could little Neddy help to chuck the Romans out?
I ran to see where he had gone and stopped in great surprise
At the unexpected crowd that met my startled eyes:

Neddy, my donkey, was there right in the middle
Of some people who were putting their cloaks on him like a saddle.
Then as I watched, they lifted up a man, and I could hear,
As they put him up on Neddy's back, a loud and mighty cheer.

The cheers grew as they set off to Jerusalem.
The people threw their cloaks down so my Ned could walk on them.
Suddenly I realized just what I was seeing:
This man was riding into our great city like a king!

Dad was right! Our king was here! I shouted too: 'Yippee!'
He'd overpower the Romans and he'd set Judea free!
The crowds were shouting praises for the marvels they had seen
And blessings on this king. But I thought—what does it all mean?

I stopped in mid-cheer, thinking, Hang on—something isn't right.
A king should have a war-horse and be dressed up for a fight.
Judea would need a mighty army to secure release
And donkeys—aren't they ridden just by men of peace?

I stared at Jesus and I wondered what he had in store
For all of us. Was he a man of peace or man of war?
How could one man hope to fight the Romans on his own?
And would the priests and Pharisees want this Jesus on the throne?

The cheers they echoed round him, and the loud hosannas rang
While Neddy plodded onwards with the quiet shabby man.
The crowd were waving palm leaves—it was quite a sight to see:
A king, like David, riding home in joyful victory.

But later in the week, somehow, those cheers turned to boos
And shouts of 'Does he think that he's the true King of the Jews?'
He let them kill him! Yes, he chose his pain and suffering!
That isn't my idea of a great and glorious king.

Reproduced with permission from *The Gospels unplugged* published by BRF 2002 (1 84101 243 2)

Jesus angry in the temple

LUKE 19:45–48; MATTHEW 2112–13; MARK 11:15–17; JOHN 2:13–17

Mark writes:

After Jesus and his disciples reached Jerusalem, he went into the temple and began chasing out everyone who was selling and buying. He turned over the tables of the moneychangers and the benches of those who were selling doves. Jesus would not let anyone carry things through the temple. Then he taught the people and said, 'The Scriptures say, "My house should be called a place of worship for all nations." But you have made it a place where robbers hide!'

The chief priests and the teachers of the Law of Moses heard what Jesus said, and they started looking for a way to kill him. They were afraid of him, because the crowds were completely amazed at his teaching.

We don't often see Jesus angry, but when he visited the temple and saw the rot that had set in there, in the house he loved so much, he blew his top. We often see anger as a negative feeling, but sometimes it can be the driving force to make vital changes. The episode is sometimes called 'The cleansing of the temple'. Cleansing, cleaning, housework—it put me in mind of my sisters-in-law who hate to see dirt in their houses.

In this verse, the director of a cleaning firm burns with a similar (if light-hearted) fury against what he sees to be outrageously wrong. Can you think of a situation where you have needed a good blast of fury to get a wrong put right?

House a mess? No need to fuss!
Get on the blower to Mops R Us!
The only firm to guarantee
To leave you top-to-toe dirt-free.
How do we do it? Here's the key—
It's not just a job or, worse, hobby.
It's our vocation, a raging passion,
A driving force, a wild obsession:
The sight of dirt just drives us wild.
We burn to clean what's been defiled—
The sight of grime makes our blood boil.
Dust and cobwebs make us howl;
Grubby toilets send us mad,
And in the fridge, if food's gone bad,
We wail and growl and gnash our teeth!
Slovens quail to see our wrath!
Dirt is foul! It means decay!
So purge it out without delay!
Give us filth and you'll discover
How much like swords are mop and hoover.
We wage war on foul bacteria
We will bleach your whole interior,
Scrub you down from inside out,
Sweep and mop and sponge throughout:
Your kitchen thick with rancid grease,
Your carpets all alive with fleas,
Your bathroom stains of ancient yuck,
Oh let us in to blast this muck!
We burn with anger to detoxify,
Purify and scour and scorify.
Your walls will gleam and glow and shine,
Your windows sparkle—how divine!
The air you breathe will smell of roses,
'Twill be a treat for fresh-picked noses.
You'll start afresh, just as you should,
Your loathsome rot is gone for good!
Your house is cleaner than a whistle,
Bottomed out! Yes, it's official!
When we see dirt we know no rest,
So call us in! 'Cos we're the best!

The sheep and the goats

When the Son of Man comes in his glory with all of his angels, he will sit on his royal throne. The people of all nations will be brought before him, and he will separate them, as shepherds separate their sheep from their goats.

He will place the sheep on his right and the goats on his left. Then the king will say to those on his right, 'My father has blessed you! Come and receive the kingdom that was prepared for you before the world was created. When I was hungry, you gave me something to eat, and when I was thirsty, you gave me something to drink. When I was a stranger, you welcomed me, and when I was naked, you gave me clothes to wear. When I was sick, you took care of me, and when I was in jail, you visited me.'

Then the ones who pleased the Lord will ask, 'When did we give you something to eat or drink? When did we welcome you as a stranger or give you clothes to wear or visit you while you were sick or in jail?'

The king will answer, 'Whenever you did it for any of my people, no matter how unimportant they seemed, you did it for me.'

Then the king will say to those on his left, 'Get away from me! You are under God's curse. Go into the everlasting fire prepared for the devil and his angels! I was hungry, but you did not give me anything to eat, and I was thirsty, but you did not give me anything to drink. I was a stranger, but you did not welcome me, and I was naked, but you did not give me any clothes to wear. I was sick and in jail, but you did not take care of me.'

Then the people will ask, 'Lord, when did we fail to help you when you were hungry or thirsty or a stranger or naked or sick or in jail?' The king will say to them, 'Whenever you failed to help any of my people, no matter how unimportant they seemed, you failed to do it for me.'

Then Jesus said, 'Those people will be punished forever. But the ones who pleased God will have eternal life.'

Jesus told people often about God's kindness and love. But he also told people about judgment. The Christian view of life includes a time when God will judge everything that we have done on earth—not a very popular idea in today's society, where so often people say, 'Anything goes' and 'It's fine as long as it works for me'. Jesus talks in Matthew 25 about dividing people into two groups. And what divides them is the way they have treated even the least important of God's people.

What difference would it make to the way you live your life if you believed you would meet God face to face at the end of it? What sort of people does Jesus mention as needing help? Have you ever helped anyone in any of these situations? Can you think of any stories where someone great disguises himself or herself as someone poor to see how they will be treated?

I gawped at the richness of the kingdom there at hand.
'Hang on, Lord,' I said, as I observed it.
'You've put me by the door that leads to life for evermore
By the looks of it, it seems to be the country of my dreams!
But what on earth did I do to deserve it?'

Food

He flung his arm around me and the angels stood and cheered.
He smiled, 'It's no wonder they all shout hoorays!
For when I needed food, you fed me. And then you'd
See that I was thirsty too and bring me water. Oh yes, you
Looked after me in such a lot of ways.'

Drink

'Um…' I started, but he was still counting out the times
I'd helped him: 'Yes, you welcomed me, a stranger.
When I was cold and bare, you gave me clothes to wear.
It was you who helped me, surely, when I was sick and poorly,
And you visited my jail, despite the danger.'

I got a word in edgeways—'But Lord, when did I do that?
I've never done a single thing for you!'
'Oh yes, you did, each time you helped the smallest child of mine,
Each time you gave kind treatment even to the unimportant,
By helping each of them you helped me too!'

'And what about those people over there?' I dared to ask.
'The ones with shoulders hunched and eyes downcast?'
'Well, what do you think? They never gave me food or drink,
Never visited or clothed me; never took the time to know me;
Never gave me even one Elastoplast.'

medicine

'When did we fail to help you?' the peevish people cried.
'We've never seen you hungry, sick or lonely!
We'd have loved to care for you if there'd been occasion to!
The problem's never arisen of seeing you in prison.
If only we had seen you there, if only!'

care

'You still don't understand,' he sighed, 'I've still not made it clear.
I'm talking 'bout my people, can't you see?
Every time you failed to care for my people anywhere—
Whom you saw time and again, facing trouble, sorrow, pain—
When you failed to help them, you failed me.'

Reproduced with permission from *The Gospels unplugged* published by BRF 2002 (1 84101 243 2)

The widow's offering

MARK 12:41–44; LUKE 21:1–4

Mark writes:

Jesus was sitting in the temple near the offering box and watching people put in their gifts. He noticed that many rich people were giving a lot of money. Finally, a poor widow came up and put in two coins that were worth only a few pennies. Jesus told his disciples to gather around him. Then he said:

'I tell you that this poor widow has put in more than all the others. Everyone else gave what they didn't need. But she is very poor and gave everything she had. Now she doesn't have a penny to live on.'

Jesus must have been getting very fed up with the rich, intellectual Pharisees plotting and planning and asking 'clever' questions. As he sat in his beloved temple, he was watching the crowds putting gifts for God into the 13 trumpet-shaped boxes of the treasury. To his delight, among all the wealthy givers, he saw a widow—someone who would have been the poorest of the poor in those days—putting a paltry penny or so into the collection box. Jesus saw the gift the way God sees it, not the way the sneering rich might see it, and he knew just how much those two coins meant to that widow. 'It ain't what you give, it's the way that you give it.' Can you think of a time when somebody has given what looks like a tiny amount (of money, time, kindness or effort) but which, when you look at it through God's eyes, you realize is actually a humungous amount? Was the poor widow foolish to give away what she could have spent on herself?

Which children's verse does the structure of this poem remind you of?

This is the smile of Jesus.
(draw a smile on your face with a finger)

This is the widow, humble and poor
(put hands together humbly and hunch shoulders)
Who caused the smile of Jesus.

This is the cloth woven all night
(spread out hands as if holding a piece of cloth)
By the widow humble and poor
Who caused the smile of Jesus.

These are the two tiny copper coins
(mime dropping two tiny coins from between fingertips)
Earned by selling the cloth woven all night
By the widow humble and poor
Who caused the smile of Jesus.

These are the rich with their handfuls of gold
(spread out arms and show bags of gold in both hands)
Who laughed at the two tiny copper coins
Earned by selling the cloth woven all night
By the widow humble and poor
Who caused the smile of Jesus.

This is the size of the widow's gift
(make a huge circle in the air with arms)
Compared with the rich with their handfuls of gold
Who laughed at the two tiny copper coins
Earned by selling the cloth woven all night
By the widow humble and poor
Who caused the smile of Jesus.

Foot-washing

JOHN 13:1–15

It was before Passover, and Jesus knew that the time had come for him to leave this world and to return to the Father. He had always loved his followers in this world, and he loved them to the very end…

Jesus knew that he had come from God and would go back to God. He also knew that the Father had given him complete power. So during the meal Jesus got up, removed his outer garment, and wrapped a towel around his waist. He put some water into a large bowl. Then he began washing his disciples' feet and drying them with the towel he was wearing.

But when he came to Simon Peter, that disciple asked, 'Lord, are you going to wash my feet?'

Jesus answered, 'You don't really know what I am doing, but later you will understand.'

'You will never wash my feet!' Peter replied.

'If I don't wash you,' Jesus told him, 'you don't really belong to me.'

Peter said, 'Lord, don't wash just my feet. Wash my hands and my head.'

Jesus answered, 'People who have bathed and are clean all over need to wash just their feet. And you, my disciples, are clean, except for one of you.' Jesus knew who would betray him. That is why he said, 'except for one of you.'

After Jesus had washed his disciples' feet and had put his outer garment back on, he sat down again. Then he said:

'Do you understand what I have done? You call me your teacher and Lord, and you should, because that is who I am. And if your Lord and teacher has washed your feet, you should do the same for each other. I have set the example, and you should do for each other exactly what I have done for you.'

Can you think of a time when somebody important has done a job that you had thought would be beneath them? Jesus wanted to show his followers how to be a leader. Is the Christian idea of leadership more to do with power and authority or with serving other people?

My brother went to the dump today,
Outside the town, up on the hill
Where the heaps of rubbish steam and smoke
And the stench of garbage makes you choke
And he watched a man killed.

He said, 'Adam, c'mon, it's a great day out.
Everyone should see it, everyone who can.
It's a great example when they end up dead,
Those rotten crooks.' But I shook my head.
You see, I knew that man.

I'd seen him last night there with his mates
In the upstairs room of my father's inn.
Dad had said to look after them good
And I'd taken them up the Passover food,
The lamb, the bread, the wine.

But I was so tired, you see, that day,
Been on my feet from dawn till night
Roasting the lambs for the Passover feast
Making the bread without the yeast—
That I forgot to wash their feet.

It's the slave's job, see, when they come inside.
Down on your aching knees you get
To hold cool water in a bowl,
And wash, then wipe down with your towel
Those dust-grey feet, with dried-on sweat.

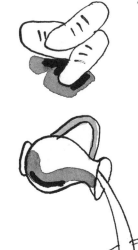

And I forgot. And served the wine
And hung right back and watched them eat.
Those mates of his, they loved that bloke,
They hung on every word he spoke,
But no one said they'd wash his feet.

Then through my sleepiness I found
Myself with Jesus face to face.
'Give me your towel and bowl,' he said,
And grinned, and cuffed me on the head.
'I'll have to take your place.'

He wrapped my towel around his waist,
No sound but the water's lap and splash.
You could have heard a heart beat
As he knelt at his friends' feet
To wash.

When he was done, he sat back down
And smiled at me and all the others.
'Do you see how I've behaved?
I'm your Lord and I've been your slave.
So do the same for all your brothers.'

He took my place, that mighty man.
I should have knelt—he knelt instead.
So I wouldn't go when I heard them say
It's Jesus being killed today.
I reckon a great man's dead.

Reproduced with permission from *The Gospels unplugged* published by BRF 2002 (1 84101 243 2)

Peter's betrayal

When the going gets tough

MATTHEW 26:47–75; MARK 14:53–72; LUKE 22:54–62; JOHN 18:12–27

Luke writes:

Jesus was arrested and led away to the house of the high priest, while Peter followed at a distance. Some people built a fire in the middle of the courtyard and were sitting around it. Peter sat there with them, and a servant girl saw him. Then after she had looked at him carefully, she said, 'This man was with Jesus!'

Peter said, 'Woman, I don't even know that man!'

A little later someone else saw Peter and said, 'You are one of them!'

'No, I'm not!' Peter replied.

About an hour later another man insisted, 'This man must have been with Jesus. They both come from Galilee.'

Peter replied, 'I don't know what you're talking about!' At once, while Peter was still speaking, a cock crowed.

The Lord turned and looked at Peter. And Peter remembered that the Lord had said, 'Before a cock crows tomorrow morning, you will say three times that you don't know me.' The Peter went out and cried hard.

Have you heard the expression 'a fair weather friend'? It must have been great to be one of Jesus' friends—to be chosen as one of the special twelve in front of everybody, to have some of his power to do miracles, to be known as a VIP when Jesus rode into Jerusalem in a triumphant procession. But what about when things got more difficult, dangerous? How did his close friends react?

My best friend Emma had to find accommodation outside college after the first year, and I had the choice whether to stay safe in college rooms or go with her into the scary world of rented flats and find somewhere together. I took the easy option and let her go on her own. And I still feel bad about it, fifteen years later. Have you ever felt let down by a friend when you most needed them? Or have you ever let a friend down yourself? Do you see yourself as a 'tough' person?

What expression do you imagine was on Jesus' face when he turned and looked at Peter? Why do you think Peter cried?

Tough! Tough as old boots, I am! As tough as years of hauling nets, heaving up the sails and straining the oars against the currents can make a man. It's a man's job, fishing! A job for a real man! You've got to be hard; you've got to be strong. You've got to be a he-man with arms like ships' masts that can brace against half a ton of fish and drag them safely in. You've got to have nerves like seasoned timbers, courage that will stare out the devil himself. And even if you're so afraid in that fragile little boat, on that great monstrous sea, that you want to cry like a baby, for Pete's sake, don't do it! Not in front of the crew. Big boys don't cry and all that. You'd lose face, wouldn't you? Stand up to your fear! You're a man's man. You can face anything.

But on solid ground, in the dark of the night, when all that's been asked of you is that you stand by your mate, when there's no crew member in sight… that's when you find out how tough you really are.

When a girl spots you and says, 'Hey, weren't you with that Jesus they've just arrested?' And everyone turns round and stares at you—a tidal wave of eyes—and you know that if you say 'yes', they'll arrest you too, and what good would that do? So you mutter, 'Jesus? Jesus who?' and stumble out of the ring of firelight.

And then a pilgrim eyes you up and points a finger: 'You're one of those trouble-makers!' he accuses. And you can't see which way the wind will blow, and you don't understand what's going on in there with those high priests, and you run for harbour for the moment: 'No! No! You've got it wrong!' And you slide away into the shadows.

And later still, when the talk's got heated and you can see the tide's turned against Jesus and the current of opinion's running strong against him, another bloke points at you and says, 'This chap must have been with Jesus. They both come from Galilee!' And self-preservation kicks in before you can even think, and your mouth shouts out: 'I don't know what you're talking about!'

And that cock-crow! That no one else even noticed! And at that moment, the guards dragged Jesus out into the courtyard and he turned and looked at me across the crowd. And clear as if he was saying the words that very moment instead of three hours ago, I heard his voice: 'Before the cock crows, you will say three times you don't know me.'

And I ran and ran. And I cried my guts out. So who's the tough guy now?

Reproduced with permission from *The Gospels unplugged* published by BRF 2002 (1 84101 243 2)

Crucifixion

The quiet man

MATTHEW 27:31–55; MARK 15:22–41; LUKE 23:26–48; JOHN 19:16–42

Mark writes:

A Roman army officer was standing in front of Jesus. When the officer saw how Jesus died, he said, 'This man really was the Son of God!'

Actions speak louder than words. Compare the power in words, in silence and in physical violence. The Roman centurion would have been used to crucifying criminals—it was all in a day's work for a soldier in an occupied country. He was used to them screaming, swearing and cursing with the pain. But in Jesus' quiet death, the centurion saw someone who was different. He saw the hidden message in the crucifixion. What Jesus had said during his life in words, he now reinforced with his final quiet action. Can you see the hidden message in this account of Jesus' crucifixion?

When is it right to protest? When is it right to stay silent? Have you ever been in a situation where someone silent turned out to be the strongest?

It's just another execution for the centurion.
Looks with hardened eyes at the crowds come to hurl abuse
On this quiet man's death.
Very quiet he is, for a criminal, thinks the centurion.
Everyone else has come with witty words:
You could call down angels to rescue you!
Or perhaps you're not the Son of God after all,
Up there on the cross? Father, forgive them.
They don't know what they're doing.
Hasn't put up much of a fight for the Son of God!
Into your hands I commit my spirit.
Son of God? Who are you kidding?
Most would have been swearing long ago. On and on the crowds yell,
Until the quiet man dies with quiet words. The Roman
Centurion silences the crowds: 'Without a doubt
He was the Son of God.'

Resurrection

Mary's story

MATTHEW 28:1–10; MARK 16:1–11; LUKE 24:1–12; JOHN 20:1–18

John writes:

Mary Magdalene stood crying outside the tomb. She was still weeping, when she stooped down and saw two angels inside. They were dressed in white and were sitting where Jesus' body had been. One was at the head and the other was at the foot. The angels asked Mary, 'Why are you crying?'

She answered, 'They have taken away my Lord's body! I don't know where they have put him.'

As soon as Mary said this, she turned around and saw Jesus standing there. But she did not know who he was. Jesus asked her, 'Why are you crying? Who are you looking for?'

She thought he was the gardener and said, 'Sir, if you have taken his body away, please tell me, so I can go and get him.'

Then Jesus said to her, 'Mary!'

She turned and said to him, 'Rabboni.' The Aramaic word 'Rabboni' means 'Teacher'.

Jesus told her, 'Don't hold on to me! I have not yet gone to the Father. But tell my disciples that I am going to the one who is my Father and my God, as well as your Father and your God.' Mary Magdalene then went and told the disciples that she had seen the Lord. She also told them what he had said to her.

The single most important claim that Christianity makes that separates it from every other religion is that Christians believe Jesus died and came back to life. Why do you think Jesus appears to a woman first after he comes back from the dead? After all, women weren't considered reliable witnesses in a court of law! Mary might have said some words like these to the despondent followers of Jesus just after she had met him in the graveyard on that first Easter Sunday.

Shut up! Shut up! OK, Thomas, so I'm only a woman! But you've got to listen to me, you've got to hear this! Look, Matthew—are you Jesus' followers, or aren't you? Well, then! Shut it and listen!

Some of you know me—I'm Mary, Mary Magdalene. Oh, don't look like that! I might have been ill once—out of my mind, even. But since I met Jesus, I've changed! Anyway, that doesn't matter now, because this is too…

You think I've gone barking mad again, don't you? Because I saw him die? I can see you swapping glances. Well, yeah, I did see him die, and no, I'll never be able to forget it. It was the worst day of my life. But today…! Today's the best day of my life! I'll never forget this one either!

Hang on—let me just get things straight in my mind… OK! The last you heard was them putting Jesus' body into the tomb, yeah? One of those graves carved out of the rock. They wrapped his body in linen cloths and put him in this grave. They rolled an enormous rock in front of the door to keep it safe. You with me so far? Nothing special about that, was there? Happens whenever someone dies. We couldn't do anything else for him—it was the day of rest. So I went off with the other women to get the embalming spices ready for today.

Well, I couldn't sleep last night. So this morning, before it was properly light I ran to the graveyard and found the grave. But… someone had rolled the rock away! I went in… Not a sausage. The grave was empty. Like… completely empty! Just the linen strips lying on the stone shelf and no sign of Jesus' body. What was I supposed to do? I ran to get Peter and John and they came and looked and muttered in low voices, but they just went away again…

The sun was up by then, and the dew was shining in the grass like teardrops, and I was crying. Dead furious, I was! Couldn't they have left his body alone after all they'd done to him already? And I heard this voice: 'Why are you crying?' I thought it was the caretaker, so I said, 'If you know where they've taken his body, you tell me, then I can go and look after him.' And this bloke said, 'Mary…' And when I turned round, there he was! It was Jesus! Really Jesus! In the flesh! All alive!

Can you imagine it? We talked… and talked… Couldn't stop gassing—there was so much to find out—so much to say—like he'd come back after a long holiday somewhere, not like he'd been dead at all! Then he told me to come and tell you what's happened. So here I am! And…

Oh dear. Just looking at your faces, I can tell what you're thinking.

You think I'm stark raving bonkers, don't you?

Reproduced with permission from *The Gospels unplugged* published by BRF 2002 (1 84101 243 2)

Emmaus road

LUKE 24:13–35; MARK 16:12–13

Luke writes:

That same day two of Jesus' disciples were going to the village of Emmaus, which was about eleven kilometres from Jerusalem. As they were talking and thinking about what had happened, Jesus came near and started walking along beside them. But they did not know who he was.

Jesus asked them, 'What were you talking about as you walked along?'

The two of them stood there looking sad and gloomy. Then the one named Cleopas asked Jesus, 'Are you the only person from Jerusalem who didn't know what was happening there these last few days?'

'What do you mean?' Jesus asked. They answered:

'Those things that happened to Jesus from Nazareth. By what he did and said he showed that he was a powerful prophet, who pleased God and all the people. Then the chief priests and our leaders had him arrested and sentenced to die on a cross. We had hoped that he would be the one to set Israel free! But it has already been three days since all this happened.

'Some women in our group surprised us. They had gone to the tomb early in the morning, but did not find the body of Jesus. They came back, saying that they had seen a vision of angels who told them that he is alive. Some men from our group went to the tomb and found it just as the women had said. But they didn't see Jesus either.'

Then Jesus asked the two disciples, 'Why can't you understand? How can you be so slow to believe all that the prophets said? Didn't you know that the Messiah would have to suffer before he was given his glory?' Jesus then explained everything written about himself in the Scriptures, beginning with the Law of Moses and the Books of the Prophets.

When the two of them came near the village where they were going, Jesus seemed to be going further. They begged him, 'Stay with us! It's already late, and the sun is going down.' So Jesus went into the house to stay with them.

After Jesus sat down to eat, he took some bread. He blessed it and broke it. Then he gave it to them. At once they knew who he was, but he disappeared. They said to each other, 'When he talked with us along the road and explained the Scriptures to us, didn't it warm our hearts?' So they got up at once and returned to Jerusalem.

Tiny moments can be as life-changing as long, slow processes—falling in love, for example, can take a life-time or happen in the blink of an eye. Have you ever experienced a moment that changed your life, your ideas or your feelings for ever? Read the story of Jesus' two friends walking sadly back home, thinking Jesus was dead. There comes a moment for them when nothing can ever be the same again.

the point
instant
moment
trice

threshold
watershed
crossroads
pivot

final fingerprint
final straw
final piece

O!

scales fall
light falls
penny falls

magic eye resolves
kaleidoscope reforms
tumbled tiles tessellate

breath stops
words start
heart burns

Breakfast on the beach

JOHN 21:1–19

Simon Peter said, 'I'm going fishing!'

The others said, 'We will go with you.' They went out in their boat. But they didn't catch a thing that night.

Early the next morning Jesus stood on the shore, but the disciples did not realize who he was. Jesus shouted, 'Friends, have you caught anything?'

'No!' they answered.

So he told them, 'Let your net down on the right side of your boat, and you will catch some fish.'

They did, and the net was so full of fish that they could not drag it up into the boat.

Jesus' favourite disciple told Peter, 'It's the Lord!' When Simon heard that it was the Lord, he put on the clothes that he had taken off while he was working. Then he jumped into the water. The boat was only about a hundred metres from shore. So the other disciples stayed in the boat and dragged in the net full of fish.

When the disciples got out of the boat, they saw some bread and a charcoal fire with fish on it. Jesus told his disciples, 'Bring some of the fish you have just caught.' Simon Peter got back into the boat and dragged the net to shore. In it were one hundred and fifty-three large fish, but still the net did not rip.

Jesus said, 'Come and eat!' But none of the disciples dared ask who he was. They knew he was the Lord. Jesus took the bread in his hands and gave some of it to his disciples. He did the same with the fish. This was the third time that Jesus appeared to his disciples after he was raised from death.

When Jesus and his disciples had finished eating, he asked, 'Simon son of John, do you love me more than the others do?'

Simon Peter answered, 'Yes, Lord, you know I do!'

'Then feed my lambs,' Jesus said.

Jesus asked a second time, 'Simon son of John, do you love me?'

Peter answered, 'Yes, Lord, you know I love you!'

'Then take care of my sheep,' Jesus told him.

Jesus asked a third time, 'Simon son of John, do you love me?'

Peter was hurt because Jesus had asked him three times if he loved him. So he told Jesus, 'Lord, you know everything. You know I love you.'

Jesus replied, 'Feed my sheep' … Then he said to Peter, 'Follow me!'

Have you ever had so much excitement or sadness or a mixture of the two that you feel quite exhausted? Perhaps then you go back to something safe—a sort of security blanket. (For me, it's historical romances and a mug of coffee.) Peter and the other disciples were in a similar state after Jesus came back from the dead. And Peter especially was still feeling weighed down with guilt for letting Jesus down by saying that he didn't know him. If a friend lets you down, is there no way you can trust them again? How easy is it to forgive them? Is it always the right thing to do? What if the tables are turned and it's you who lets a friend down—would you hope they might forgive you? See how Jesus and Peter worked things out. Then look up Matthew 16:17–19.

What a week us disciples of Jesus had had,
A wild rollercoaster ride—anarchy—mad!
We had seen our close friend—who we thought was our king—
Put to death on a cross. Could anything
Be worse than watching your dearest friend die?
But I was the wretchedest, because I knew I
Had betrayed him three times, had disowned him, had said
'I don't know that man!' And now he was dead.

But then he came back! Back to life! We all saw
The graveclothes, no body, no stone at the door
Of the grave. Then we saw him! Saw Jesus! Alive!
He came to us, spoke with us. I tell you, I've
Never lived through so much anguish and heartache
And then hope and joy. Now I needed a break.

I went back to what I was sure of—my boat.
Wood, canvas, nets: no questions, no doubt,
No feelings of failure—'I'm off for a fish,'
I muttered to John. 'To escape—humph, I wish!'
'We'll come too!' the others said, glad for a rest,
Glad to get back to what they knew the best.

You win some, you lose some, but that night was bad,
The worst night for fishing that we'd ever had
Except for one night three long years ago…
But that was all buried—let it stay so!

By dawn we'd caught nothing. Was this the end?
Couldn't do my old job. Couldn't stand by my friend.
I looked at the peace and the calm of the waters
And longed for a second to end it—like Judas.
Then fought to remember exactly what Jesus
Had said about finding that deep-down forgiveness
I needed. We heard a man shout through the mist:
'Hey lads, what's your catch?' 'Nothing!' James hissed.
'Then throw out your nets to starboard,' he shouted.
'There's plenty of fish there.' I grunted, 'I doubt it.'

But we threw in the nets and could not haul them in
'Cos each of the nets was filled to the brim.
John was peering across through the mist to the shore.
'Hey, Peter!' he whispered. 'I think it's the Lord!'

Could have turned my boat round and sailed quickly away.
Could have run from this man I'd deserted, betrayed.
Could have let my guilt tell me how much I should fear him.
But I didn't think—I just had to be near him!

I threw on my coat and I plunged in the sea
And staggered to where he stood laughing at me.
What we said then was between me and him—
But let me tell you, it was well worth the swim.

He'd built a small fire and we smelt some fresh bread.
'Well, bring me a few of those fish, lads,' he said.
He took them and cooked them right there on the sands
And he shared out the food with his own wounded hands.

And after we'd eaten our best meal to date
He looked in my eyes and he asked me quite straight:
'Simon, John's son, do you love me more
Than the others do?' It was then that I saw
I had to make up for the hash that I'd made.
'Yes, Lord, you know I do,' was what I said.
'Simon, John's son, do you love me?' he asked.
I swallowed. The words that I'd said in the past,
'I DON'T KNOW THIS MAN!' echoed round in my head.
'Yes, Lord, you know that I love you,' I said.
He asked me a third time, still used my old name:
'Simon, John's son, do you love me?' My pain
Welled up from inside me, I shouted: 'Oh Lord,
You know everything!' Know I'm guilty, a fraud,
A wreck of a man, but the truth still came through:
'You know everything and you know I love you!'

Only then at the third time, then could I see,
Like sight after blindness, how much he loved me.
And he talked for a bit while my guilt disappeared.
I felt his power in me—my conscience was cleared.
I was even more ready than three years ago
When he said 'Follow me!' with my whole heart to go
In his strength, not mine. It would be till the end
Of my life. And I'd die for my Saviour and Friend.

Reproduced with permission from *The Gospels unplugged* published by BRF 2002 (1 84101 243 2)

Ascension

On the hill

MATTHEW 28:16–20; MARK 16:19–20; LUKE 24:50–53

Luke writes:

Jesus led his disciples out to Bethany, where he raised his hands and blessed them. As he was doing this, he left and was taken up to heaven. After his disciples had worshipped him, they returned to Jerusalem and were very happy. They spent their time in the temple, praising God.

Hills and mountains are special places in the Bible. Think of some important events in the Old Testament that happened on mountains—Noah's boat coming to rest on Mount Ararat; God giving Moses the Ten Commandments; the temple being built on a hill. In this poem, Jesus reminds his friends about the experiences they have had together on hilltops and invites them up the last hill he will climb with them on earth.

Can you work out what each verse is talking about? Have you got a special place where you feel close to God? Do you think it's good to have somewhere 'apart' where you can think about things? Or do you think every place is a special place on God's earth?

Come up the hill.
Outside the bustle of the town,
Where you can choose—look up or down.
We are apart now
On the hill.

Come up the hill.
I taught you there,
Broke bread to share.
We walked and laughed there
On a hill.

Come up the hill.
I prayed there for you.
Learned what to do.
I went apart there
On a hill.

Come up the hill.
We met with glory,
Learned the full story.
You knelt there
On a hill.

Come up the hill.
Where the empty cross lies
Under the dark skies,
Cut off there
On a hill.

Come up the hill.
Like angels sang at my birth,
Glory in heaven, peace on earth,
Together though parted
On the hill.

Reproduced with permission from *The Gospels unplugged* published by BRF 2002 (1 84101 243 2)

Theme index

Verse forms index

Gospel references index

Stories of Everyday Saints

40 stories with Bible links and related activities
Veronica Heley

This book provides 40 five-minute read-aloud stories of people who have lived their lives for God. Each story links to a key Bible passage, includes its own prayer, has suggested activities including crafts, drama and creative writing, and shows a symbol for the saint and suggestions for songs. In the centre of the book there is a photocopiable chart where all the saints' symbols are given. The saints fall into four categories: Bible saints from the New Testament, such as St Paul; historical and legendary saints, such as St George; worldwide saints, such as St Francis of Assisi; and contemporary saints, such as Mother Teresa.

1 84101 224 6, £8.99

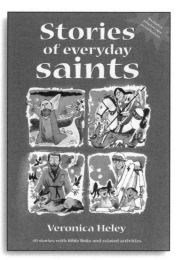

Stories to Help You Pray

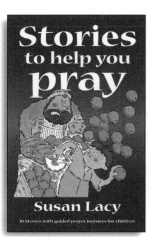

10 stories with guided prayer journeys for children
Susan Lacy

Contains ten Bible stories, each told from the point of view of a child and followed by guided meditations. The stories are taken from the Gospel accounts and set within the correct historical and social background in order to enrich the child's understanding and to help the story to come alive. Key Bible verses are included.

The meditations are followed by directed questions to facilitate the child's experience of entering the story itself and an invitation to 'look out' of the story and take its meaning into the rest of the day. All the material has been thoroughly field-tested within the normal school day with 6–10s.

1 84101 188 6, £4.99

More Stories to Make You Think

Heather Butler

Following on from the popular *Stories to Make You Think*, this book provides a further selection of topical and often sensitive subjects designed to stimulate discussion between adult and child. The author uses biblical insights and thinking time to provide an accessible entry point into difficult subjects. Each story has been researched and tested in Circle Time and PSHE at primary level and can be used either in a one-to-one situation or with a group in the classroom, church or family.

1 84101 141 X, £4.99

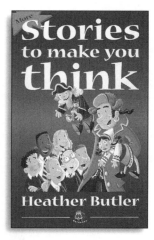

Available from your local Christian bookshop or, in case of difficulty, direct from BRF.
Tel: 01865 319700; Fax: 01865 319701; E-mail: enquiries@brf.org.uk

Visit the **brf** website at www.brf.org.uk

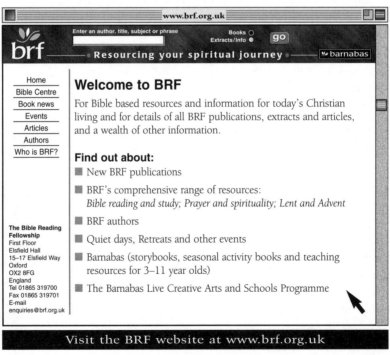

www.brf.org.uk

Enter an author, title, subject or phrase

Books ○
Extracts/Info ●

go

brf

Resourcing your spiritual journey

barnabas

Home
Bible Centre
Book news
Events
Articles
Authors
Who is BRF?

The Bible Reading Fellowship
First Floor
Elsfield Hall
15–17 Elsfield Way
Oxford
OX2 8FG
England
Tel 01865 319700
Fax 01865 319701
E-mail
enquiries@brf.org.uk

Welcome to BRF

For Bible based resources and information for today's Christian living and for details of all BRF publications, extracts and articles, and a wealth of other information.

Find out about:

■ New BRF publications

■ BRF's comprehensive range of resources:
Bible reading and study; Prayer and spirituality; Lent and Advent

■ BRF authors

■ Quiet days, Retreats and other events

■ Barnabas (storybooks, seasonal activity books and teaching resources for 3–11 year olds)

■ The Barnabas Live Creative Arts and Schools Programme

Visit the BRF website at www.brf.org.uk

BRF is a Registered Charity